Contemporary Chinese Celebrities

Asian Celebrity and Fandom Studies

Asia arguably has the world's most vibrant star, celebrity and fandom cultures, due in part to its globalized entertainment media and cultural industries and its large population base, and yet there is little sustained scholarship on this highly significant cultural and economic arena. The Asian Celebrity and Fandom Studies Series aims to meet this research gap, promoting new and innovative scholarship in Asian media and cultural studies, and screen studies, by concentrating on the most salient issues surrounding Asian stardom, celebrity and fandom.

The Asian Celebrity and Fandom Studies Series is devoted to the publication of scholarly books that critically examine star, celebrity and fandom cultures in specific Asian countries, in trans-Asian or trans-national contexts, and among Asian diasporas. The series publishes monographs, co-authored books, and edited collections. All proposal and manuscripts are subject to rigorous peer review.

Forthcoming titles:

Beyond the Male Idol Factory: The Construction of Gender and National Ideologies in Japan through Johnny's Jimusho by Yunuen Ysela Mandujano-Salazar

Livestreaming China: An Ethnography of Vulgar Boredom by Dino Ge Zhang

Series Editors: Jian Xu and Sean Redmond

Contemporary Chinese Celebrities

Moral Transgressions, Rights Defence and Public Concerns

Shenshen Cai

BLOOMSBURY ACADEMIC

LONDON • NEW YORK • OXFORD • NEW DELHI • SYDNEY

BLOOMSBURY ACADEMIC
Bloomsbury Publishing Plc, 50 Bedford Square, London, WC1B 3DP, UK
Bloomsbury Publishing Inc, 1359 Broadway, 12ᵗʰ Floor, New York, NY 10018, USA
Bloomsbury Publishing Ireland, 29 Earlsfort Terrace, Dublin 2, D02 AY28, Ireland

BLOOMSBURY, BLOOMSBURY ACADEMIC and the Diana logo
are trademarks of Bloomsbury Publishing Plc

First published in Great Britain 2024
This paperback edition published 2026

Series design by Ben Anslow
Cover image © Feng Li / Staffy via Getty Images

A catalogue record for this book is available from the British Library.

Library of Congress Cataloging-in-Publication Data
Names: Cai, Shenshen, author.
Title: Contemporary Chinese celebrities : moral transgressions,
rights defence and public concerns / Shenshen Cai.
Description: London ; New York : Bloomsbury Academic, 2024. |
Series: Asian celebrity and fandom studies | Includes bibliographical references and index. |
Summary: "Whether willingly or unwillingly, public celebrities are often the focus of
discussion of moral matters and political causes, but how does this sort of celebrity culture
function in a country such as China with a powerful central state? Celebrity Activism and
Governance in Contemporary China explores how in today's China, celebrity figures embody,
conflict with and engage with social, civil, moral and economic issues. Shenshen Cai examines
the state's governance of celebrity activism and the interplay between the propaganda
machine and the stars"– Provided by publisher.
Identifiers: LCCN 2023047274 (print) | LCCN 2023047275 (ebook) | ISBN 9781350409460 (hardback)|
ISBN 9781350409422 (paperback) | ISBN 9781350409453 (epub) | ISBN 9781350409446 (ebook)
Subjects: LCSH: Celebrities–China–Social conditions. | Celebrities–Political activity–China. |
Fame–Social aspects–China. | Fame–Political aspects–China.
Classification: LCC HM621 .C323 2024 (print) | LCC HM621 (ebook) |
DDC 920.051–dc23/eng/20231201
LC record available at https://lccn.loc.gov/2023047274
LC ebook record available at https://lccn.loc.gov/2023047275

ISBN: HB: 978-1-3504-0946-0
PB: 978-1-3504-0942-2
ePDF: 978-1-3504-0944-6
eBook: 978-1-3504-0945-3

Series: Asian Celebrity and Fandom Studies

Typeset by Deanta Global Publishing Services, Chennai, India

For product safety related questions contact productsafety@bloomsbury.com.

To find out more about our authors and books visit www.bloomsbury.com
and sign up for our newsletters.

Contents

Acknowledgements

I would like to express my sincere gratitude to Dr Emily Dunn for her ongoing support and advice during the writing and editing of this book. Emily was so patient and devoted in helping me to polish and fine-tune my arguments and writing. Without her careful and time-consuming editing of the drafts, this book would not have become what it is now.

Also, I would like to thank the Asian Celebrity and Fandom Studies series editors, Dr Jian Xu and Professor Sean Redmond, for their kind support during the review and production of the book.

Finally, I want to thank the editors from Bloomsbury Academic, Mr David Avital and Ms Olivia Dellow, for their time and support during the processes of reviewing, writing and producing the book.

Introduction

Celebrity culture in contemporary China

Celebrity culture has been a constitutive part of moral institutions, cultural trends and sociopolitical impact as China has globalized and risen to become the new economic superpower in the new millennium. Yet such was not always the case. In traditional Chinese culture and society, 'Xizi' (戏子) was a word with derogatory connotations that expressed distaste and disrespect for actors and actresses from noble and upper social cohorts and even the lower social classes. The expression 'Biaoziwuqing, xiziwuyi' (婊子无情戏子无义), translated as 'The whore is heartless, the actor does not have righteousness', reflected Chinese people's impression and representation of prostitutes and actors in ancient China. Traditional Chinese society honoured government officials, intellectuals and the gentry class, and despised businessmen, performers and prostitutes. In traditional society, all sorts of performers including Peking and local opera actors and other folk arts performers belonged to humble professions such as those of wizard (巫师), night watchman (更夫), barber (剃头匠), trumpeter (吹鼓手) and beggar (乞丐).

This humble status and treatment of performers was changed and lifted after the Chinese Communist Party (CCP) took power in mainland China in 1949. According to the CCP's directives on literature and the arts, performers were enlisted and mobilized to promote and circulate the party line. Since the beginning of the People's Republic of China (PRC), propaganda has been an innate and vital part of the CCP's strategy of political control and ideological manipulation. The state propaganda machine has been very adroit at utilizing mass entertainment to publicize official doctrine and spread party directives (Mackerras 1981; Kaikkonen 1990; Holm 1991; Link 2007; Gerdes 2008;

Webster-Cheng 2008; You 2012; Cai 2016). In particular, the CCP's method of combining ideology with the functions of folk literature and performing arts genres became a unique feature of party publicity in the post-liberation period. Chosen for their entertainment value and massive public appeal, indigenous Chinese performing arts such as crosstalk (相声), storytelling (评书) and the musical storytelling art of Suzhou (苏州评弹) were recruited by the propaganda institutions to convey party ideology and policy. The founding of the PRC in 1949 marked the beginning of a new social system, and in this new proletarian society, street performers (街头艺人), who were once exploited and discriminated against, were seen for the first time as artists and artisans (Xue 1985: 120). In keeping with the new social rules and sociopolitical reality, and to help with the propagation of the CCP's policies, street performers took an active part in political studies and worked hard to improve their political correctness.

Those performers who pioneered the integration of political propaganda in their folk-art works and performances gained unprecedented popularity and political trust from the party. For example, Hou Baolin (侯宝林), who headed the Small Group for the Improvement of Xiangsheng (北京相声改进小组) in the early 1950s, was a loyal follower of the party's literary and arts line. The Small Group for the Improvement of Xiangsheng modified many old crosstalk pieces, removing any pornographic or risqué jokes, references to inappropriate class attitudes and other ideological flaws that were originally part of the works (Link 1984: 97; Xue 1985: 124; Xiang 2008: 155), so that the content reflected the opinions of the ruling authorities. Most of the reformed works lampooned society's remnants of feudalism, eulogized the new regime and promoted optimism among the people (Ma 1980: 26). Hou Baolin was commended by the party as a 'people's artist' and active in giving performances in North Korea during the Korean War (1950–3). Such new titles and public images gained by street performers from 1949 reflected their changing social and political status in Maoist China.

The change in performers' social status and political function in modern China can be traced back to the early decades of the twentieth century, which witnessed the emergence and influence of left-wing artistic works in stimulating nationalist and patriotic sentiments and socialist revolutions. In 1930s Shanghai, there was a group of left-wing film companies, directors and actors, who passionately participated in the creation of films that reflected the social and political atmosphere of that historical period. Issues depicted included class and gender inequality, suffering of the Chinese people and anti-Japanese sentiment. Left-wing writers including Xia Yan (夏衍) and Tian Han (田汉) and directors such as Cai Chucheng (蔡楚生), Yuan Muzhi (袁牧之) and Shen Xiling (沈西苓) scripted and directed many popular left-wing films that gave birth to a generation of film stars such as Wang Renmei (王人美), Zhao Dan (赵丹) and Bai Yang (白杨). These stars enjoyed continued popularity among the public and political recognition by the CCP in socialist China. Those classic screen images of Wang Renmei in *Song of a Fishermen* (渔光曲, dir. Cai Chusheng, 1934), Zhao Dan, Zhou Xuan (周璇) and Wei Heling (魏鹤龄) in *Angels on the Road* (马路天使, dir. Yuan Muzhi, 1937), and Zhao Dan and Bai Yang in *Crossroads* (十字街头, dir. Shen Xiling, 1937) not only produced a group of film artists with superb acting but also lifted the social and political status of performers who embodied national and patriotic spirit, class struggle and the awakening of gender consciousness.

Prior to the rise of nationalist and patriotic emotion and the socialist revolutionary sentiments in 1930s China following the Japanese invasion and the arrival of Marxist theory, Chinese performers lacked social status as a result of media reporting, public commentary and rumours and established social institutions. This was the case even if they had gained unparalleled popularity among audiences and considerable income. From the beginning of the 1930s in Chinese film circles, there was a tradition of evaluating female movie stars by whether their performances reflected the 'true character' of the actress; it was thought that their public personae should be congruent with their private selves. Female stars were expected to be modern subjects whose professional roles reflected their authentic selves (their *bense*本色), and the media representation of this authenticity should display uniformity between their private life and public image (Chang 1999: 152; Wing-Fai 2014: 71). The example of famed 1930s Shanghai actress Ruan Lingyu (阮玲玉) would support this argument as there were many similarities between Ruan's off- and on-screen lives. For example, her poor family background and gloomy fate matched the conditions of many of the humble and unfortunate female characters she played, such as the prostitute role in *Goddess* (神女, dir. Wu Yonggang, 1934) and the pitiful mother character in *Small Toys* (小玩意, dir. Sun Yu, 1933). Ruan Lingyu, coincidentally, committed suicide because of widely circulated rumours and slander about her marriage, which mirrored the final choice of the female character she played in one of her most successful films *New Women* (新女性, dir. Cai Chusheng, 1934). In *New Women*, the suicide of the female lead, Weiming, was caused by the stress of living with illness and without a job or income. The constraints of living under conservative power, the trifling with affections by the profligate sons of the rich families and the slander penned by the tabloid journalists mirrored many of the real-life experiences of Ruan Lingyu. Ruan Lingyu's suffering and death provide a typical example of the career dilemmas and moral vulnerabilities confronting Chinese performers, which reflect the reality of the entertainment world in contemporary China and which are under examination in this book.

While performers and actors gained unprecedented and unique social status and political recognition in the Maoist era, some of them were also persecuted, purged and implicated in political movements because of their class background and roles they played in films and other performing arts genres. For example, during the Cultural Revolution (1966–76), the national style of Peking Opera was appropriated and transformed by the CCP (partly under the organization and instructions of Jiang Qing 江青, who was Mao Zedong's third wife and a member of the Gang of Four) into a popular mass recreational tool to be used to sell the party's political doctrines and ideologies to the people. During the peak of the Cultural Revolution, the Eight Model Operas (八台样板戏), which called for and celebrated continuous class struggle, became almost the only entertainment source available to the public. For this reason, performers who emerged from these classic revolutionary opera works enjoyed unanimous fame among the Chinese people, which consolidated the social and political status of performers as people's artists. Though the widespread popularity of those performers did not necessarily ensure enormous financial income in Maoist China, it marked a breakthrough in the sociopolitical status of contemporary Chinese performers.

While some performers gained gigantic honour for their participation in socialist revolutionary artistic creations, some encountered totally different fates during the 'tumultuous ten years' of radical social transformations and political activism. For example, famous actress Yang Likun (杨丽坤), who starred in the lead female role in the romantic movies *Five Golden Flowers* (五朵金花, dir. Wang Jiayi, 1959) and *Ashima* (阿诗玛, dir. Liu Qiong, 1964), became an object of criticism during the Cultural Revolution because these films were deemed 'poisonous weeds' that promoted 'the supremacy of love'.

They were accordingly labelled as 'reactionary' films and were boycotted and banned. Yang Likun, as the female lead in these two films, was implicated in the political movements that criticized these films. She was diagnosed as having schizophrenia resulting from the persecution inflicted upon her during the Cultural Revolution, which further led to her career breakdown, unhappy marriage and premature death. Similar to Yang Likun's experience, the Huangmei Opera master Yan Fengying (严凤英) was accused of being a 'beautiful villain' who spread feudalism, capitalism and revisionism and served as a secret agent for the Nationalist Party (KMT; 国民党); therefore, Yan was denounced many times in public meetings that led to her taking of her own life in 1968.

In Yang Likun and Yan Fengying's cases, it is not difficult to discern that in the early stages of socialist China, performers' fate was unavoidably intermingled with and woven into the sociopolitical tapestry of Maoist China. This fashion waned in the post-Mao and post-revolutionary era, during which performers and celebrities enjoyed more freedom in regard to professional and personal life choices, moral obligations and cultural and sociopolitical participation. During the relatively loosened cultural and political environment and atmosphere of the Deng Xiaoping (邓小平) era and the Jiang Zemin (江泽民) and Hu Jintao (胡锦涛) eras, performers and celebrities were given more room to create their roles, challenge traditional and established moral rubrics, express views on civic issues and contribute to political activities. Since Xi Jinping (习近平) took over reign of mainland China in 2013, moral and political surveillance over celebrities and stars and the general public have become more common and severe. Under the reign of Xi Jinping and his followers, a left turn has become increasingly apparent in the economic, moral, cultural and political domains. Thus, contemporary Chinese celebrities and stars, who have become nouveau riche during the ongoing economic and social transformations, have also become objects and prisms of economic rectification and moral and sociopolitical discipline.

The contemporary Chinese public displays an ambiguous and paradoxical response to celebrities and stars, particularly those audiences of older generations. On one hand, it no longer single-mindedly admires or condemns performers and celebrities with reference to the political situation; this is because China's entertainment industry and culture have become increasingly mature and tolerant. On the other hand, while enjoying the recreational products brought to them by celebrities and stars, Chinese audiences also hold a love–hate sentiment towards this new, nouveau riche social echelon. In other words, Chinese people somehow feel uneasy with the contemporary celebrities' monopoly on economic, cultural and sometimes even political resources. For example, in present-day China, some top stars can easily earn tens of millions of yuan in remuneration for their performances in TV drama shows, reality shows or a single movie – all despite the fact that many younger-generation stars do not have excellent performing skills. Some celebrities plunge into the sea of business and exhaust their mental energy trying to build up connections with influential business people and high-level government officials in order to further their business ambitions; others fish for political capital in exchange for better career opportunities. All these realities have challenged and refreshed the public's knowledge about the entertainment circle in modern-day China and helped to train their critical thinking and ability to participate in and comment on social, civic and political issues.

For example, it is almost beyond the commoner's imagination that a pop star or an A-list actor could earn up to one million yuan for their performance in a single episode of a TV drama, while ordinary Chinese people can hardly earn several thousand yuan per month, even in first-tier cities like Beijing, Shanghai and Guangzhou. Similarly, celebrities and stars can easily afford houses and apartments in posh suburbs of Beijing and Shanghai; in contrast, wage earners in Beijing have been pushed to live beyond the fifth ring road (dozens of kilometres away from the city centre) by skyrocketing house prices. Though it is common knowledge that Hollywood stars can earn tens of millions of US dollars for their performance in blockbusters, people still show concern that such a momentous income gap exists in a socialist country that supposedly stresses equal distribution of wealth. In recent years, Xi Jinping has repeatedly restated China's commitment to communist values: Common prosperity is the prosperity of all the people, not the prosperity of a few people . . . common prosperity is the essential requirement of socialism and an important feature of Chinese-style modernization – a refrain which was first propagated along with Deng Xiaoping's Opening Up policy at the end of 1970s. 'Wealth flaunting' (炫富) and 'wealth hatred' (仇富) have become buzzwords and topical social phenomena in today's China, emerging from the popular impression that China's nouveau riches make huge profits through shady and illegal ways such as bribery and participating in factional political struggles. Further, the rich people's unscrupulous flaunting of their wealth through consuming goods from expensive international labels and purchasing private boats and aeroplanes makes them a target of hatred among Chinese people. Many Chinese people even harbour a 'totalitarian nostalgia' for the Mao era, which although materially inadequate at least delivered a degree of social and economic equality. Some top film stars such as Zhang Ziyi (章子怡) 'are easily opened to criticism as the envied, yet denigrated, idols of hedonistic capitalist consumption when compared with the nostalgically imagined model citizens of an era defined by socialist collectivism and production' (Jeffreys and Edwards 2010: 18).

Those 'common prosperity' slogans and financial equality ostensibly pursued by Xi Jinping and his followers seem to indicate a left turn in the economic and social domains in order to consolidate the legitimacy of Xi's administrations in particular and the Communist Party's rule in China in general. Consequently, together with business tycoons and billionaires, contemporary celebrities and stars have become the political targets as representatives of the *nouveau riche* social cohort in post-revolutionary China. Back in 2017, Xi Jinping promised to tackle 'extreme wealth' at the beginning of the second term of his reign; however, it was only in late 2021 that the CCP Central Committee promised to enforce 'reasonable adjustments to excessive income'. It is widely rumoured that China's most famous pop star Zhao Wei (赵薇) built up close connections with Chinese billionaire Jack Ma (马云), who was targeted after Ma dared to criticize CCP regulators for stifling tech sector growth (Siedel 2021). After Zhao Wei and her husband were banned from entering China's financial markets for 'tying a white wolf with bare hands' (空手套白狼),[1] Jack Ma drew a demarcation line with Zhao Wei by clarifying with the media that he and Zhao were not acquaintances at all. Here, it is hard to say whether Jack Ma's loss of favour from the party led to the exposing of Zhao Wei's immoral practices in the financial market (in other words, whether Zhao was implicated in Ma's case by virtue of extremely complicated bonds and factions in China's political, business and entertainment circles); however, it is evident from Zhao and Ma's case that no matter how much wealth and popularity one accrues in contemporary China, it is still power that decides one's fate and fame.

Observably in present-day China, celebrities, their public image and behaviours, and debates about them have become a conduit through which topical and controversial social, cultural, economic and political issues are identified and discussed among Chinese people. From domestic gender roles to the leftover women phenomenon; from extramarital affairs and mistresses to soliciting prostitutes; from 'effeminate' aesthetics (Nancy Boy culture) to sexual harassment; from tax evasion to 'white gloves' incidents; and from participating in democratic demonstrations to voicing concerns about environmental pollution or economic and political corruption, contemporary Chinese celebrities and stars have made themselves a focus of public debate and comment.

In Mandarin, the phrase 'white gloves' (白手套) has financial and political connotations. The innocuous-sounding code word generally refers to a broker or party that launders dirty or corrupt money under a seemingly lawful front: dirty hands concealed by a pair of white gloves. This new cultural expression, coined in Taiwan, has become a cultural buzzword as rampant corruption has been exposed at all levels of the bureaucracy in mainland China. In his book *Red Roulette* (红色赌盘, 2021), Desmond Shum (沈栋), former husband of arrested Chinese billionaire Duan Weihong (段伟红), exposed how Duan became the 'white gloves' of former premier Wen Jiabao's (温家宝) family to gain huge amounts of money. Smooth-talking Chinese business people seek opportunities to enrich themselves by leveraging ties to powerful politicians and gaining inside information, and consequently became the 'white gloves' of senior government officials.

'White gloves' scandals have also spread to the entertainment circle of present-day China. Zhao Wei and her husband Huang Youlong (黄有龙) have been widely reported to have powerful backstage supporters who enabled them to develop 'the white wolf speculative thinking mode' and to defraud Chinese people in the financial market. Commentators suggest that the exposure and punishment of Zhao and her husband's immoral practices in the financial market might have been linked to the CCP's crackdown on Jack Ma and his corporation, Alibaba, as Zhao and her businessman husband were close allies of Ma. Resulting from the exposure of these practices, Zhao has been labelled a 'tainted star' and her name has been removed from all the works she starred in on major Chinese video platforms like Tencent Video, iQiyi and Youke (Zhang 2021).

Seemingly, in present-day China, just as there is 'a pair of white gloves' for every corrupt government official, there is also a mistress behind every one of them. Many celebrity figures also join this army of mistresses of government officials. It is common knowledge that during the Cultural Revolution, many sent-down female urbanite youths had sex with local CCP cadres in exchange for permission to return to their hometowns or assignment of lighter work duties (Jeffreys 2006: 171).[2] Likewise, in contemporary cases of corruption, many CCP officials have traded power and sex. The women normally receive a promotion following their affair with a leader in their organzsations or with other powerful high-ranking government officials. An indirect way of trading in power and sex is coordinated by business people, who hire the services of female sex workers to offer as gifts to CCP cadres and officials in exchange for business opportunities (Jeffreys 2006: 169). Similarly, some underlings of high-ranking CCP officials serve as sex brokers, introducing pretty women – and in some cases, celebrity and stars – who provide sexual services to their supervisors and leaders.

One such case publicized in 2014 involved Zhou Yongkang (周永康), the former minister of Public Security and secretary of the Political and Legislative Affairs Committee of the CCP Central Committee, who was also a former member of the Politburo Standing Committee of the CCP Central Committee. Zhou retired in 2012, was arrested in 2013 and executed in 2015.[3] Zhou reportedly had affairs with two China Central Television (CCTV) hosts, one of whom was promoted to the position of deputy director of the Information Centre of the Political and Legislative Affairs Committee of the CCP Central Committee. Further, it is rumoured that the former vice-minister of the Ministry of Public Security acted as a liaison to enable the affairs between Zhou and the CCTV hosts. In recent decades, many famous Chinese television presenters and singers have been revealed to be concubines or mistresses of high-ranking corrupt officials. Some people even joke that CCTV has become the imperial harem of Zhongnanhai (中南海), which is the central headquarters of the CCP and the Government of the PRC. It is reported that of the high-profile cases involving government officials at a ministerial level, almost every case investigated entailed some form of trading in power and sex (Jeffreys 2006: 161). On one hand, these scandals reveal the extreme moral decadence of high-ranking CCP officials. They also reflect the desperate pursuit of power, reputation and materialistic enjoyment by these famous women of China.

Undeniably, in the entertainment circle of present-day China, there are more and more scandalous celebrities and tainted stars. Their behaviour and scandals have become dinner-party fodder for the Chinese people, the spotlight of media coverage and the object of government criticism and crackdowns. Communism seems to be striking back as the Chinese censors are busy setting things straight. State-run media outlets have been spreading messages such as 'raise the threshold to become a celebrity', 'virtue before artistry' and 'the rewards of a moral society' (Siedel 2021). Moral quality, standards and monitoring have been resumed to help maintain the government's control over all the aspects of Chinese society. This may also be understood as a type of manipulation enlisted by the CCP to divert the public's attention away from its own corruption and illegitimacy of reign. Following this logic, celebrities and private business owners have become scapegoats as Xi orchestrates a left turn in the economic, social, cultural and political spheres to maintain and consolidate the legitimacy and reign of the CCP government.

Further, critics provide insight into the government's rectification of 'effeminate' fashion (Nancy Boy culture) in the entertainment circle, which aims to re-masculate Chinese men in order to make them ready for the military retake of Taiwan. In today's world, while globalization has been a continuing and dominant trend in international economic and cultural interactions and cooperation, new geopolitical groups and powers have formed because of the United States' strategy to return to Asia and compete with China for dominance in the Asia Pacific region in particular and the world in general. Most recently, Russia's invasion of Ukraine has further demonstrated the unstable security situation in Europe and the American-led NATO's recession from ensuring the military safety and political stability of Europe. Evidence increasingly suggests that it is entirely possible that the world will be governed under a new Cold War logic given the ever-deteriorating relations and intense competition between the two world superpowers – China and the United States. Moreover, Russia's desire for revenge for decades of America-led sanctions, its ambitions to revive itself as a global superpower and China's growing military ambitions in the West Pacific region all indicate the increasing Cold War logic and the ever-growing complex and perilous geopolitical conditions.

All these external uncertainties make the Chinese government vigilant towards any future military conflict. In addition, given the negative impact and side effects of the Covid pandemic on the Chinese economy and international image; the unprecedented slowdown in China's annual GDP figures; the increasing unemployment rate; the social turmoil caused by gender imbalance;[4] and corruption in officialdom and factional struggles at the top level of politics, the Xi Jinping administration certainly needs stronger public security and armed forces to maintain both internal and external stability. Thus, a nuanced type of mobilzsation and propaganda has been implemented in the entertainment circle that boycotts the Nancy Boy fashion, which is believed by the CCP to be emasculating and feminizing young Chinese men. Obviously, this trend of 'weakening' and 'feminizing' Chinese men does not satisfy the party's need to strengthen its military power and serve as a deterrent. This pragmatic consideration and demand from the government involves reforming, disciplining and monitoring celebrities' public image and personas and reshaping China's popular culture landscape more generally. This surveillance, regulation and manipulation from the propaganda machine of the CCP show how government directives cascade to the entertainment industry and affect the individual career development of celebrities and stars, which moreover illustrates that the CCP has again leveraged tight control over the entertainment circle and celebrities as it did in the early stages of socialist China.

Another reason for the government to tighten its control over celebrities and stars is that some sporting celebrities, TV drama and film stars, and celebrity hosts of news programmes, reality shows and talk shows have started to articulate concerns about controversial issues including environmental pollution, the premature deaths of disadvantaged peasants and workers, bribery and corruption in the economic system and sexual harassment in officialdom. As mentioned earlier, performers and actors in ancient China belonged to the lowest social class and few received education except training in their professional performing art; thus, they were despised and discriminated against not only by the noble class and intellectuals but also by Chinese people. Therefore, those performers in traditional China were not charged with arousing the wisdom of the people, which was the job of intellectuals; instead, their main job was to reinforce the moral admonitions and constraints that were embedded in their performances. During the Anti-Japanese War (1937–45) in the Republican era, several famous Peking Opera masters such as Mei Lanfang (梅兰芳) and Cheng Yanqiu (程砚秋) refused to perform for the Japanese captains and soldiers in order to awaken Chinese people's national spirit to resist the Japanese invasion. During the Socialist period from 1949, performers and artists developed their professional careers under the directives of the party and were dedicated to spreading the party policy and lines (though some were still persecuted and purged during peaks of incessant political movements such as the Cultural Revolution). During the Opening Up era, many actors and artistic workers obtained the opportunity to receive higher education that enabled and enriched their social functions. Under this relatively tolerant and open social and political atmosphere, actors and celebrities were eager to show their concern for established and socialist moral mores and social institutions, which marked their eagerness in representing and setting examples for the Chinese people.

The famous Chinese actress Liu Xiaoqing (刘晓庆) has been one of those pioneers within the ranks of outspoken celebrities. Liu Xiaoqing became a household name in 1980s China by virtue of her excellent performing skills, which brought her many national awards. However, she noted in her two autobiographies *My Road* (我的路, 1983) and *My Confessions* (我的自白录, 1995) that the recognition of her acting talents did not initially bring her extra wealth; she earned only about fifty yuan per month in the mid-1980s. Despite being a nationally famed film star, she was unable to provide well for her parents, owned no decent (let alone fashionable) clothes, could not afford to eat meat and following her divorce did not have a Beijing home. These impoverished circumstances led Liu Xiaoqing to realize that economic affluence and a comfortable lifestyle were as important to her as career objectives, fame and popularity. This transformation in thought reveals that Liu Xiaoqing had realized that to be a productive and exemplary actor who was loved by the people and promoted by the state did not mean one was able to satisfy one's own material and individual pursuits. Liu Xiaoqing did not want to be an 'iron girl' (铁姑娘)or a 'model female worker' (劳模)as eulogized by the Mao regime; she required more from her efforts than just socialist morality. Consequently, Liu Xiaoqing joined the moonlighting (走穴) fashion that was popular among singers and actors during the initial stage of Deng Xiaoping's economic reforms and she became a self-employed business person (个体户).[5]

Liu Xiaoqing's endeavours in both her film career and business, which are recounted in detail in *My Road* and *My Confessions*, stimulated and inspired many Chinese viewers in their search for a more affluent life and in their efforts to realize their individuality. As well as embodying great determination, the Liu Xiaoqing phenomenon bore an apparent feminist imprint. In *My Road*, which was first published in 1983 when the majority of Chinese women still thought conservatively, especially in regard to their gender and family roles and moral beliefs, Liu openly calls for Chinese women to care about more than just their marriages; instead, she writes, they should consider their own lives and careers as their priority (Liu 1983). In both pre-modern and socialist China, Chinese women were exploited and suppressed by the patriarchal and state feminist discourses, which required them to bow to either traditional doctrines or national or communist causes. However, in Liu Xiaoqing's case, no matter whether they were traditional customs and norms or official socialist directives and rules, she would not follow them unless they concurred with her own heart. Liu Xiaoqing's loves and marriages are often compared with those of the British-American film star Elizabeth Taylor. Taylor's multiple marriages and love affairs did not reduce her audience appeal; on the contrary, they are generally regarded as evidence of the actress's open-mindedness towards marriage and love, and her bravery and courage in pursuing an unconventional life. In a well-known talk show that interviews Chinese and foreign politicians, business people and celebrities (*Yang Lan Fangtanlu* 2012), Liu Xiaoqing stated: 'Marriage as a social contract opposes human nature; however, it guarantees the rights of women. Is it a good choice to lead a single life? One can still enjoy love, affection and all the contents of married life, but without being subject to the constraints of marriage.' In another popular talk show programme hosted by China's transgendered celebrity Jin Xing (*Jinxing Xiu* 2015), Liu Xiaoqing revealed that she was 'forced' to marry her four husbands and that she herself did not want to get married at all.

Just as Liu Xiaoqing's rebellious behaviours and opinions challenged traditional moral codes and social institutions such as gender roles and marriage, some contemporary Chinese celebrities have extended their attention to controversial and sensitive economic, social and political issues, which have long been considered by the CCP government as taboo and therefore banned from public view and comment. Under the current suffocating climate in the media industry under the reign of the Xi Jinping administration, the once-popular newspaper *Southern Weekly* (南方周末) – which has been famous for its in-depth, authoritative and insightful revelations and reporting of controversial and sensitive social events – together with many freelance investigative journalists has been silenced or had its business licence revoked. Thus, celebrities' public voicing of concern and their shouldering of the responsibility of public intellectuals have become vital to the Chinese people's ability to access and participate in public debate of social, cultural and political topics.

Dyer has observed that 'Celebrities are a set of ideas and representations in which people collectively make sense of the world and the society in which they live through the media texts that create "stars"' (Dyer 1998: 2). Following Dyer's observation, I argue throughout this book that in today's China, celebrities not only serve as a lens reflecting topical sociopolitical issues and controversial cultural phenomena in contemporary China; they also configure and refresh cultural norms and moral codes, stimulate thinking and debates about social and civil issues, and participate in economic and political changes and progressions.

The book will focus on the interaction and confrontation between celebrity and social, cultural and political topics and trends in present-day China. In so doing, it will illustrate and clarify the complex, interdependent and provocative nature and characteristics of the bonds between official culture and celebrity culture within contemporary China's entertainment circle. Through exposing and analysing these connections and altercations between mainstream culture and celebrity culture, the focus of the book is celebrity governance and activism in contemporary China. Through studying the moral transgressions, rights defence and public concerns campaign and movements initiated and implemented by contemporary Chinese celebrities, the book examines different cohorts of Chinese celebrities including scandalous celebrities, celebrity public intellectuals, sports celebrity, feminist celebrity and internet celebrity. By analysing typical cases of these celebrity activists, the focus of the book revolves around how contemporary Chinese celebrities and star figures act to arouse and attract the public's attention to reconfigure the moral bonds and institutions of current China, to defend their civil and human rights, and to participate in the discussion and campaigns of public concerns.

The book has seven chapters. Chapter 1 has provided an introduction to celebrity culture in contemporary China. Chapter 2 focuses on scandalous celebrity and celebrity governance in present-day China, which highlights the persistence of the moral bindings and institutions of traditional and socialist China and how the CCP government enlists these moral constraints to manipulate and control the Chinese people. Chapter 3 examines celebrity intellectuals including writers, journalists and university professors and their endeavours to raise the public's awareness and participation in civil and human rights campaigns that challenge the rule of the CCP over mainland China. Chapter 4 studies some recent celebrity figures in the sporting world who have boldly challenged the CCP's legitimacy of rule in mainland China, though their efforts did not generate much impact among the Chinese citizens. Chapter 5 focuses on celebrity feminist rights defenders and activists in mainland China who have drawn women's rights issues to the public's attention. Chapter 6 examines influential internet public activists and their courageous behaviour and reporting to expose the mailaises of the CCP's government; Chapter 7 provides a conclusion for the book.

From different perspectives, the book's chapters study various celebrity figures and cohorts and the challenges they pose for the CCP's management, control and manipulation of mainland Chinese citizens. Further, the book's chapters uncover celebrity figures' voices and efforts to promote the media freedom, civil and human rights of Chinese citizens, and to question the political system and legitimacy of rule of the CCP in mainland China. Overall, the book's goal is to foreground the voices and activism of contemporary Chinese celebrities regarding their challenges to the CCP government and its rule in mainland China, and their impacts and effects on the Chinese people. The body of the book uses different cohorts of celebrities and case studies to support and realize this goal.

Scandalous celebrities are chosen as the central topic of **Chapter 2** because they serve as prisms that reflect those social, moral and economic stigmas emerging since the Opening Up period, and the CCP's policy and governance in the economic, sociocultural and ethical domains. In the past decade, scandalous celebrities and stars have become a lens through which present-day China's social malaises, economic controversies and moral decline have been revealed and become a focus of public attention and debate. Further, scandalous celebrities are often enlisted by the Chinese government for their usefulness in the continuing negotiation of the party's needs, challenges and failings. Serving as negative examples or points of reference, the party adjusts and updates its financial, moral and sociocultural directives and policies through its governance of celebrities. To some extent, celebrity figures can therefore be regarded as a wind vane in reading the changing trends of the party's guidelines and ideology aiming at consolidation of its rule and legitimacy. This chapter analyses those scandalous celebrities and tainted stars in the Sinophone entertainment world, who once enjoyed huge popularity among their fans.

There was a tradition in the early stages of socialist China that performers and celebrities served as moral models for audiences to emulate and admire. 'Excellent in both performing skills and moral integrity' (德艺双馨) was commonly used to describe a performer or artist in the cultural rhetoric of socialist China; however, in the past decade, owing to the emergence and convenience of social media and self-media devices, more celebrities have been exposed of misconduct and crimes including tax evasion, money laundering, extramarital relations, frequenting prostitutes, rape and drug taking. These misbehaviours of the scandalous celebrities serve as bad examples that lead the party to modify its regulations and policies in the moral, economic and sociocultural domains. Case studies of this chapter include Liu Xiaoqing (刘晓庆), Fan Bingbing (范冰冰), Huang Haibo (黄海波), Wen Zhang (文章), Wu Xiubo (吴秀波) and Wu Yifan (吴亦凡). These case studies were chosen because they serve as the most representative examples in their respective fields regarding moral transgression, economic misconduct and cultural and social controversies that the Chinese government tightens its control of through its governance over celebrities.

The other focus of the book is on the emerging fashions of celebrity activism in current China. In the political and social atmosphere of today's China, almost all kinds of activism – whether in the fields of human rights, women's rights, civic rights or political rights – are constrained. The CCP is unleashing a regressive left turn and is tightening its control over morality, escalating its surveillance and disciplining of media practitioners and industry and intensifying its punishment of human rights defenders and political dissidents. The majority of public intellectuals and human rights lawyers and political activists have been silenced, detained or persecuted. Thus, the emergence and development of celebrity activism in today's China aiming at bringing about political and social change is of considerable importance to the Chinese people and the Chinese nation. In this book, I employ a broad sense of celebrity that includes famous writers, influential hosts and reporters, popular movie and TV stars and directors, star sportspeople and professors, who act as active embodiments and advocates of moral reconfiguration, economic makeovers, social liberation, the rights of women and political changes, which in turn manifest the developing trajectory of celebrity activism in China today.

Nayar has expressed that 'Celebrity activism is a part of the democratization of public renown, through shared ideological and political commitment with people around the world and enabling (or fitting into) communities of interest' (2021: 7), and Redmond states that 'Celebrity exists through forms of signification and as over-arching and textually specific discursive formations' (2018: 35–6). Moreover, 'Celebrity representations carry the range of politicised values and meanings that are attached to their image when in circulation. Celebrity representations are never neutral: they carry the discourses, concerns, inequalities and dreams of the contemporary age' (Redmond 2018: 36). Famous social critics such as Theodor Adorno and Max Horkheimer suggest that celebrity is the product of the 'culture industry' and acts as a coercive force which shapes society according to oppressive ideologies that favour the powerful elite over the general public (Meyers 2009: 891). In this book, however, I contend their negative view and demonstrate how contemporary Chinese celebrities challenge the dominant and repressive ideologies and social mores through voicing their concerns about the Chinese general public and the Chinese nation. As noted by Larkin, 'those who are well known in our society, particularly in the areas of entertainment and sports, possess a magical charm that captivates the hearts and souls of most Americans . . . [and] these athletes and entertainers (including musicians, actors and all others performers) dominate twenty-first century notions of celebrity' (Larkin 2009: 156). Further, 'soft news' related to these charming and popular figures helps to 'democratize information', which increases the chances that the average Americans will learn about issues facing their nation (Larkin 2009: 162). Larkin's observation on the American case also applies to the Chinese context. In the following chapters of the book, I will focus my discussion on contemporary Chinese celebrity activism in several domains including human and civic rights, women's rights, political change and political rights.

Chapter 3 studies a group of film and TV stars, crosstalk performers, celebrity hosts, journalists and writers, highlighting their participation in and dedication to addressing public concerns and in constructing a civil society in which people can freely articulate their opinions regarding social inequality and other controversial and sensitive sociopolitical issues. It is common knowledge nowadays that compared with the Republican era (1912–49) and the cultural hits of 1980s China, many present-day Chinese intellectuals are either enlisted by the party or silenced by the state apparatus; thus, they rarely function as public intellectuals. Some public intellectuals are actually selected, cultivated and endorsed by the party; thus, these pseudo public intellectuals become centres of public attention. This dynamic marginalizes those true public intellectuals and deprives political dissidents and rights-defence lawyers of discursive power. In this context, some celebrities and stars step forward bravely as human and civil rights activists to shoulder the responsibility of a genuine public intellectual. This chapter focuses on those based in mainland China, who risk their fame and fortune when they speak up for the Chinese people and the disadvantaged because they could be libelled and pressured, and their performances, works and shows could be banned by the Chinese government. Case studies of this chapter include Chai Jing (柴静), Jin Xing (金星), Cui Yongyuan (崔永元), Fang Fang (方方), Yan Geling (严歌苓) and Zhou Xiaozheng (周孝正). These case studies were chosen because they represent the most influential and respected famous public figures in contemporary China. They have intervened in such important incidents as the SARS and Covid-19 pandemics and the war in the Ukraine, affecting the Chinese public's understanding of and attitudes towards these issues.

Chapter 4 examines China's sports celebrities and their words and deeds that challenge the political stability of contemporary China. Sports celebrities were hailed as national heroes during the early period of socialist China. Whether shooting or track and field athletes, those who became world champions for the PRC were honoured as heroes of China, and promoted by the CCP propaganda machine as showing Chinese people's courage and persistence in the face of blockades from countries that harboured hostility towards the PRC. In the early 1970s, China's ping-pong diplomacy helped to break the ice with America in the political, diplomatic and cultural domains. Sports seems to have a natural bond with Chinese politics in regard to their nationalist appeal and uniting power. For example, China's lacklustre performance in soccer has always been something of a national trauma. However, Chinese soccer's 'scar' status in the hearts of many Chinese people has proved its unifying strength and nationalist appeal as a sports activity. In recent years, sports celebrity has increasingly been associated with national sentiments in both the official media and the populous voices of nationalist advocates. On the other hand, there have also emerged sports stars who have exposed a culture of corruption in the sports circle. These stars question the legitimacy of the Chinese government as they consider the chaos in the micro sports circle to mirror the corruption and pandemonium in the macro social and political domains. This voicing of concerns from the sports celebrity illustrates new ways that sporting stars could contribute to the building of an equal and sound society under the rule of law. Case studies of this chapter include Hao Haidong (郝海东), Ye Zhaoying (叶钊颖) and Peng Shuai (彭帅). The case studies were chosen because of their uniqueness and rarity and because sports stars' open defiance of the Chinese political system poses an unprecedented challenge to the party's rule.

Chapter 5 discusses contemporary Chinese women's rights-defending activities and movements involving celebrities and stars. In recent years, Chinese women have displayed improved awareness of their rights. Instead of sticking to the traditional 'good wife, wise mother' role, more and more Chinese females prioritize their own career aspirations and development over marriage and family duties that have been forced upon them by traditional and socialist ethical mores. Rather, Chinese women speak up for themselves regarding their choice not to get married and give birth to children; they defend themselves against physical and emotional bullying and violence, including rape and sexual harassment; and have participated in the Chinese version of the #MeToo movement. Moreover, as represented by female celebrities and stars, female rights activists in China have launched their own sexual liberation campaign. This overthrew the traditional and repressive understanding about sexual relationships, in which men forever occupied the dominant position; instead, Chinese celebrity writers and media practitioners call for Chinese women to consume men rather than being consumed by men. Case studies of this chapter include Muzi Mei (木子美), Hong Huang (洪晃), Li Jinglei (李靓蕾), Chen Shu (陈数) and Yang Liping (杨丽萍). These case studies were chosen because they reflect the most controversial debates over women's rights and celebrities' usefulness in safeguarding them in current China.

Chapter 6 discusses internet celebrities (*wanghong*) – specifically, their participation, function and influence in Covid-19 news reporting and the most recent protests against Covid-19 lockdowns in mainland China. Case studies of *wanghong* independent reporter Chen Qiushi (陈秋实) and 'Li Laoshi is not your teacher' (李老师不是你老师, nickname of a Chinese *wanghong* independent reporter who posts on Twitter) will be included in this concluding chapter. As an enormous social and civil force in present-day mainland China, some Chinese *wanghong* involve themselves in defending human and civil rights and protest against the authoritarian rule of the CCP. Chen and Li's cases are representative, and worth reading as a constitutive part of Chinese internet celebrities' participation and contribution in building a public sphere and promoting citizens' rights and political change in modern-day China.

Chapter 7 summarizes the research findings of the book.

In summary, the topic of Chapter 2 demonstrates how the CCP initiates and implements changes in the moral, economic, social and cultural arenas through celebrity governance. Chapters 3 to 6 have been selected to reflect celebrity activism in different arenas of contemporary China and thus to provide a comprehensive and dynamic depiction and interpretation of celebrity activism in China today. The overall contribution and value of this book is that through its substantive focus on the Chinese celebrity scene, the book maps out a depiction of contemporary Chinese celebrity governance and activism.

Scandalous celebrity and celebrity governance

In the past decade, scandalous celebrities and stars have become windows through which present-day China's social malaises, economic controversies and moral decline have been revealed and become a focus of public attention and debate. As a privileged sociocultural stratum in contemporary China, celebrities and stars serve as conduits through which topical and controversial social, cultural and economic topics and discussions are exposed and reviewed. As Hermes, Kooijman and Nayar point out:

> Celebrities may have charisma bestowed on them by the magic of being in and of the media; in everyday life they are held to account for their usefulness in the ongoing negotiation about society's (or, indeed, the nation's) needs, burdens, challenges and faults, whether as example (good or bad) or points of reference . . . [and] The making of an affect-driven intimate public demonstrates not only celebrity power but also the values placed upon certain conditions, events and acts: suffering and victimhood, resistance, survival, triumph, and so forth. (Hermes and Kooijman 2016: 495 cited in Nayar 2021: 5)

Further, Penfold (2004: 300) argues that 'Celebrities showed themselves to be an important rallying point for society, where the public can be bound together in a sense of community and togetherness similar to that experienced during a national disaster or war'. Scholars have noted that certain celebrities and stars represent 'certain values and ideologies at particular times, embodying and often resolving the contradictions ordinary people experience in their everyday lives under capitalism. . . . . . stardom has the capacity to challenge or critique a culture's ideological shibboleths' (Dyer and McDonald 1998 cited in Frame 2020: 345–6).

These observations also apply to Chinese celebrities and stars regarding their social and cultural representations and functions at different historical conjunctures. For example, the financial well-being enjoyed by modern Chinese celebrities and stars was unparalleled by performers and stars of previous eras. In the Republican era, film stars and master folklore arts performers including Peking Opera masters Mei Lanfang (梅兰芳) and crosstalk master Hou Baolin (侯宝林) earned enormous amounts of money out of their performances that meant they could easily afford a luxurious lifestyle and a house in Beijing. Up to the socialist era, though the social status of the performers and artists was enhanced and endorsed by the CCP, their living standards could not be compared with those living in the Republican era, let alone to those of present-day China. Maoist China emphasized egalitarianism, aiming to wipe out class and financial differences. This demotivated many performers and stars regarding improving their living through their career development and endeavours. In the case of Liu Xiaoqing in the post-Mao era, her national fame as a film star could not provide her a comfortable lifestyle. After Liu worked on a series of mainland and Hong Kong co-produced films directed by the famous Hong Kong director Li Hanxiang (including *Reign Behind a Curtain*/垂帘听政, 1983, *The Burning of Yuan Ming Yuan*/火烧圆明园, 1983, and *The Empress Dowager*/一代妖后, 1989), she recognized the material and financial differences enjoyed by the mainland actors and those based in Hong Kong, which further stirred her to make more income and to improve her financial welfare. Liu Xiaoqing's joining in the moonlighting trend and plunging into the sea of business that emerged in the early post-Opening Up era helped her to realize her dreams.

Compared with Liu Xiaoqing's time, in the most recent decades, celebrities and stars live in an era that supports transformation of economic systems. Some people become prosperous first and comprise a nouveau riche social echelon; therefore, the income of celebrities and stars, particularly A-list actors, is determined by market demand and the audiences' preferences. Similar to those top stars in Hollywood, A-list Chinese film and TV stars can earn hundreds of millions in remuneration simply by starring in a commercial blockbuster or a popular TV drama show. It has become common knowledge that in the current entertainment industry of China, the largest part of the cost of production for a commercial movie or a TV serial is its stars' remuneration. If a star is involved in a scandal after the shooting of the movie or TV show, the production company will remove the part featuring the scandalous star, which in the worst-case scenario will lead to the re-shooting of the entire movie or TV drama. This brings gigantic economic loss for the production company. Consequently, according to the contract signed by the production company and the star, the star will shoulder at least part of the company's loss. While some audiences enjoy the visual delight brought to them by their idols in a blockbuster, other audiences have begun to ponder the skyrocketing remuneration of film and TV stars in a critical way. The public has started to consider: How was this lowest social class of ancient China elevated to the status of 'people's performers and artists' in Maoist China? And how has this privileged social cohort become the nouveau riche under the rubric of the market economy in post-socialist China?

Undoubtedly, these nouveau riche celebrities and stars bring happiness and enjoyment to audiences through their performance and enrich the cultural and recreational spare time of the Chinese people. Yet, on the other hand, their seemingly unimaginably high income has caused jealousy and hatred among the public, as in contemporary Chinese society there is a widespread psychological resentment of the rich. Particularly among those generations who were born in Maoist China in the 1950s and 1960s, there is a sense of nostalgia for the totalitarian Mao era. Aspects of the current economic, political and social conditions of China contribute to the nostalgia for the early stages of socialist China. For example, nostalgia serves as a hope and ideal with which to counterbalance the negative consequences of the combination of political and economic patterns in post-socialist, post-revolutionary China (Lu 2007: 131). Nostalgia is culturally fabricated to cater to the emotions of contemporary Chinese audiences who harbour a longing for the revolutionary past and spirit. Recent economic restructurings, together with social and cultural change, have generated social disruptions that contest the leadership, authority and legitimacy of the CCP regime. It is political reasoning prompted by natural disasters, economic uncertainty, mass protests against corruption and the Tiananmen Square crackdown that has triggered the fashion for top-down, state-led nostalgia (Zhu 2008: 34). Apart from this top-down nostalgia craze, there also exists a bottom-up version: the phenomenon of totalitarian nostalgia evident in the revival of Mao's Little Red Books, his image and iconic items of the Cultural Revolution. This includes a Red wave of commercially packaged revolutionary songs, plays and movies that not only flood the market but also feed a certain nostalgia for the totalitarian past (Cui 2003: 51). This phenomenon is considered 'a roundabout way of protesting the social stratification caused by the economic reforms which were initiated by Deng Xiaoping and his followers at the end of the Cultural Revolution' (Honig 2003: 175).

In the current era of Xi Jinping's rule, a combination of the top-down and bottom-up types of totalitarian nostalgia has become increasingly apparent as the Xi administration repetitiously emphasizes the importance of common prosperity and the general public appeals for more equal and transparent economic, social and political systems. As typical representatives of the nouveau riche social echelon, celebrities and stars have been a focus of public attention and debate regarding their wealth and their methods of accumulating it. Back in the late 1980s, which witnessed the Tiananmen demonstration, the appeals and demands of the college students, intellectuals and everyday people were to boycott official profiteering, corruption, social inequality and the privileges enjoyed by specific social classes. However, accompanied by the brutal military crackdown on this democratic protest, the situation within the business world and entertainment circle deteriorated in the following decades. Within the entertainment circle, there existed tax evasion that resulted from government dereliction of duties, bribery of government staff and corruption within officialdom. Moreover, given that more and more stars earned remuneration that a commoner would find hard to imagine, and they intentionally avoided tax on their huge amount of income, some Chinese citizens started to question: Is this phenomenon also a characteristic of the so-called socialist China?

The most famous cases that ignited the general public's interest and anger include those involving famous singer Mao Amin's (毛阿敏) and popular film star Liu Xiaoqing's tax evasion. Liu Xiaoqing was sentenced and jailed between 2002 and 2003 on charges of major tax evasion by the companies she ran or was affiliated with as a legal representative. Tax evasion was rife among Chinese celebrities and stars during the Opening Up period. According to the investigations into Liu Xiaoqing's companies, they had evaded huge sums of tax through accounting indiscretions since 1996. In contrast to her previous titles such as 'the nation's best actress' and 'business tycoon', Liu Xiaoqing secured a fresh public image as China's best-known tax dodger. As the typical representatives of China's nouveau riche social classes, celebrities and stars became the target of fury and disparagement because of their illegal means of getting rich, which is regarded by the Chinese people as a microscopic reflection of the macroscopic injustice and corrupt social reality of present-day China.

As noted by Larkin and Drezner, 'celebrities must be aware that the media will always push to expose the man behind the curtain . . . [and] Americans are addicted to celebrities because we like to see them on top – but we also enjoy their fall' (Drezner cited in Larkin 2009: 168). These scholars' observation about American audiences' attitude towards celebrities and stars applies to Chinese audiences as well. The Chinese public's interest and enjoyment in watching a star's fall from grace stems from their hatred of the rich. Celebrities and stars act as agents of China's nouveau riche social cohorts, of which many become wealthy through immoral or illegitimate practices including tax evasion and building connections and bribing government officials. As observed by Ching-Ching Ni, author of reports regarding Liu Xiaoqing's case that were published in the *Los Angeles Times* in 2002, the CCP authorities picked Liu Xiaoqing as they were looking for a high-profile deterrent for tax evasion among China's new rich. The Liu Xiaoqing incident attracted huge media and public attention and panicked neophyte capitalists from entrepreneurs to entertainers, who raced to pay their taxes (Ni 2002).

Back to the early decades of the Opening Up period, in Chinese people's mindset, paying taxes was still a new concept given their low-income levels. Thus, those celebrities and stars who got rich first became the touchstone of a newly introduced economic system and the government's monitoring, control and discipline of the new rich social cohorts and the ever-widening gap between the rich and the poor. For celebrities and stars, their disadvantage compared with real business tycoons was their popularity and the public profile they had established through songs they sang, film and TV drama roles they played, and advertisements they featured in and endorsed. All these were sociocultural signifiers and assets that could easily bring them recognition or notoriety. The Liu Xiaoqing phenomenon revealed that in contemporary China, although popularity and fame could be cashed in on and help one to become rich faster, political governance, discipline and monitoring of wealth and fame formed the political-cum-wealth/fame rules of practice.[1] In other words, celebrities and stars could be used as a weathervane when the government intended to loosen or tighten its economic policy to either encourage or punish those people who get rich faster than the rest of the Chinese people. Though arguably, celebrity and stars may be considered scapegoats of industry and business magnates, who achieve wealthy status through more complex and contemptuous methods (Ni 2002), celebrities and stars have become the weathervane of the economic and political rectifications and purges of modern-day China.

Mao Amin was not as brave and calm as Liu Xiaoqing when confronting charges of tax evasion. Mao, a veteran pop singer, was known as the 'Big Sister' (大姐大) of contemporary China's music circle. However, this famous woman fell from grace in 1989 as a result of her involvement in under-the-table payments for her performances. Consequently, Mao was ordered to pay back 15,000 yuan in tax and was fined 34,000 yuan for her misconduct. From 1994 to 1996, Mao Amin once again was caught for tax evasion and this time the amount was about 100 million yuan. Almost the biggest celebrity scandal of that period, Mao collapsed and attempted suicide on multiple occasions but failed for various reasons. Mao then went abroad to avoid public attention and denunciation as she was rated as one of the ten least popular stars of those years by the audiences. However, it seemed that the Chinese audience was either oblivious to Mao's transgressions or extremely tolerant of their idols. After she had made her reparations of roughly 1.4 million yuan, Mao returned to her position in front of the audience and reprised her popularity and reputation from 2000. In 2001, Mao was listed as one of the thirty-six Chinese athletes and entertainers who were illustrated on a sequence of postage stamps released in assistance of Beijing's bid to host the 2008 Olympic Games – a huge honour. Gies points out that there appears to be a high level of public forbearance for celebrities who misbehave and break the law. This has given rise to worries that celebrities are bad role models who are encouraging antisocial behaviour (Gies 2011: 347).

After Xi Jinping came to power in 2013, in order to combat economic corruption, moral decline and social instability, which undermined the legitimacy of the CCP government, Xi and his administration initiated a left turn in almost all aspects of China's economic and social realms. For example, they launched the unparalleled crackdown on high-level corrupt officials, resumed the government's control of state-run factories and companies, ripped off wealthy businessmen, tightened political surveillance and media control and even endorsed a new Cold War logic. All of this would, in their estimation, help to build a more equal, stable and harmonious Chinese society. Under this overarching rubric, financial rectifications and crackdowns on disorder and illegal conduct were imposed on the entertainment industry. In 2018, an inquiry into tax evasion in the entertainment circle was instigated by the government, with a focus on investigating actors accused of signing 'yin-yang' contracts (阴阳合同). Those actors and targeted entertainment companies were accused of setting out payment terms in one contract and nominating a lower figure of repayment in another contract, which was actually signed by both parties and which was provided to tax authorities. This enabled the actors to avoid paying large amounts of tax. One of the actresses targeted was popular film and TV star Fan Bingbing (范冰冰). The whistle-blower in the case of Fan Bingbing was the celebrity TV host Cui Yongyuan (崔永元), who has been extremely popular with and respected by Chinese audiences because of his sharp viewpoints on topical and controversial social issues in contemporary China that were revealed in his TV talk show, *Tell It Like It Is* (实话实说). As one of the most successful talk show programmes that has ever been produced by CCTV, *Tell It Like It Is* enjoyed great popularity among the Chinese public and turned its host Cui Yongyuan into a celebrity presenter. However, in 2013, Cui withdrew from the show and resigned from CCTV and established his own production studio. Moreover, he also joined the Communication University of China (中国传媒大学) as a lecturer.

Cui seemed to act as a lighthouse to many conscientious Chinese celebrities, intellectuals and Chinese people who were cynical and critical towards the social inequality and corruption of contemporary China. However, it is widely rumoured that Cui developed depression because he was privy to too many shady deals going on in Chinese society and this conflicted with his conscientiousness and integrity as an intellectual, causing him great suffering. Marshall and Redmond observed that 'Even when celebrities are signified as lonely, sufferers of depression, addiction, or other addiction mental health problems, they offer us the space to collectively share so that we are not isolated sufferers. They are higher order healers and soothsayers whose wonderment lifts us up and out of ourselves so that we can be productive citizens and workers' (2016: 11).

Owing to Cui's popularity and influence among the Chinese public, China's commercial film director Feng Xiaogang (冯小刚) made a film entitled *Cell Phone* (手机) in 2003 in which Cui Yongyuan and *Tell It Like It Is* were incorporated into the storyline. One of the plot strands of the film is that a celebrity talk show host (based on Cui Yongyuan) develops an extra marital affair with a young newspaper editor (played by Fan Bingbing). This was rumoured to be based on Cui's real-life experience and negatively affected Cui's public image. However, despite the negative emotional and public influence *Cell Phone* left on Cui Yongyuan and his family, Feng Xiaogang and the scriptwriter of *Cell Phone*, Liu Zhenyun (刘震云), produced a sequel to the original film in 2005. This was intolerable for Cui and totally destroyed his relationship with Feng. Because of the disputes and lawsuits between the two, *Cell Phone 2* has yet to be released. For her repeated cooperation and good relationship with Feng Xiaogang, Fan Bingbing was implicated in the enmity and fights between Cui and Feng. Cui posted prints of files on his social media account, declaring that they were copies of separate contracts signed by Fan for the same job and that the primary disparity was the size of her remuneration. Cui's revelation of the 'yin-yang' contract was later proven to be true, and Fan was fined 800 million yuan for her transgression. Fan's case was only the tip of the iceberg as the 'yin-yang' contract is a very common practice in the entertainment industry of present-day China. Many celebrities and stars were deterred by Fan's case as the 'yin-yang' contract not only destroyed Fan's acting career but also turned her into a public enemy by association with the immoral and corrupt rich social echelon. In this way, she has been virtually denied any opportunity of making money in the entertainment world.

In recent years, another representative celebrity tax evasion incident has involved another popular actress, Zheng Shuang (郑爽), who was issued a 299 million yuan fine. Consequently, TV dramas, films and reality shows with Zheng's participation were all banned from showing. Besides Liu Xiaoqing, Mao Amin, Fan Bingbing and Zheng Shuang, other celebrities and stars have been exposed of acting immorally and illegitimately in the financial market as business people and investors had been implicated in the punishment of commercial moguls by the government by virtue of their close bonds with the magnates. In this sense, Zhao Wei (赵薇) may serve as a typical example to clarify the relations between celebrity and the business circle of current China. Zhao Wei, a middle-aged pop actress, singer and director, married a businessman and became a billionaire celebrity. Besides acting in films and TV shows, in recent years, Zhao Wei also directed several commercial films and documentaries. Relying on her public persona as a youth idol, Zhao Wei successfully sought and built connections with China's wealthiest business people, such as Wang Jianlin (王健林) and Ma Yun (马云; Jack Ma). Zhao became close friends with Wang's wife and won her favour, and the couple's good relationship with China's top business circle undoubtedly helped them in developing their own business empire. Along with the rapid increase of their wealth because of Zhao's popularity and connection with business tycoons, she and her husband developed 'the white wolf speculative thinking mode', which practices fraud in the financial market, and resulted in investigation and punishment by relevant Chinese financial departments, though the fines and punishment involved were widely believed to be not severe enough.

When Zhao's misconduct in the financial field was first exposed, it was widely rumoured that she would not be punished because she had powerful supporters behind the scenes in high-level Chinese officialdom. Observably, there exist complex relationships among business magnates, stars and high-level government officials, who might all be targeted and implicated in economic crackdowns and political fights. In other words, there may exist a top-down domino effect as when a high-level government official loses power and influence, the business people and stars relying on his or her support and protection will be implicated as well. Trading on her celebrity image and popularity, Zhao easily became close to Ma Yun and participated in Ma's business ventures. Ma is the billionaire founder of the Alibaba Group (阿里巴巴). He irritated the CCP government following his critique of state bureaucracy and subsequently disappeared from public life for three months. Arguably, Zhao was implicated because of Ma's loss of favour with the CCP government, and this was why her business practices and assets began to attract close monitoring by the relevant government bodies. Zhao's investments have incurred a series of lawsuits, including her early stake in Alibaba Picture Group, which is a film company affiliated with Ma Yun's Alibaba Group. As a result of being a scandalous star, Zhao has had her name erased from Chinese video platforms; moreover, Zhao's fan page on China's most influential social networking site, Weibo, has been taken down, and this scandalous news of Zhao topped the trending lists on Weibo the day her online presence was scrubbed. It is also rumoured that these scandals revolving around her made Zhao temporarily leave the country to avoid the media scrum.

Zhao Wei and Ma Yun's cases may be just one in the recent round of cracking down on the nouveau riche class under the reign of Xi Jinping, who has repeatedly said that common prosperity is the indispensable prerequisite of socialism and a critical characteristic of Chinese-style modernization. Xi has pointed out that it is vital to adhere to the policies of marketization and rule of law, and to coordinate the avoidance and resolution of key financial perils. It seems that Xi associates private billionaires with such financial risks when increasing wealth disparity undermines his call for common prosperity. Further, concentrations of wealth are identified as pressures on the power of the CCP, which has enforced rigorous new guidelines on business investment, ownership and control. When Xi returned to power for a second term in 2017, he promised to tackle 'extreme wealth' and to enforce 'reasonable adjustments to excessive income' in order to win trust and favour from the public and thereby consolidate his rule. Thus, when private business tycoons are suppressed, it is reasonable to believe that 'It is not all about economics. It's also about power' (Seidel 2021).

The scandal surrounding Zhao Wei has triggered a series of crackdowns within China's entertainment circle that have consolidated the party's determination to monitor and initiate changes to China's entertainment culture. The supervisory clampdown has followed the release of a policy guide, 'Implementation Outline for the Establishment of a Rule of Law-Based Society', which authorizes the formation of 'moral norms' as 'legal norms' (Seidel 2021). The enactment and implementation of this 'rule by moral norms' can be traced back to the former president Hu Jintao's era. For example, contemporary crosstalk master Guo Degang was targeted by the CCP as a dissenter of the Counter Three Vulgarities Campaign because of the vulgar comical elements he regularly performed in his crosstalk works and his exposé and satire of the morbid and corrupt social reality of present-day China. In July 2010, Chairman Hu Jintao explicitly expelled the Three Vulgarities from the cultural domain of contemporary China (Hu 2010). The following month, the CCP's Propaganda Department launched a new cultural campaign, the Counter Three Vulgarities Campaign, at which time Guo Degang and his crosstalk productions were labelled as 'vulgar'. Guo Degang argued that the government picked on whatever he did as he became a famous representative of the Three Vulgarities. CCTV aired a programme on its News Studio segment that criticized Guo Degang. Although his name was not mentioned outright in the programme, it was clearly directed at him: 'Between the merits and trash of the profession, he chose the latter; between the healthy trends and unhealthy trends, he chose the latter; and between personal antagonism and a public figure's duty, he habitually resorted to personal antagonism. This public figure's secular, vulgar and low camp behaviour is so ugly' (Peng 2010: 68). As a result, two of Guo's most helpful disciples announced their withdrawal from the Deyun Club – the crosstalk club Guo had established to put on commercial crosstalk and other folk art performances – and many major bookstores were ordered to remove videos and products associated with Guo Degang from their shelves. Entertainment programmes on local TV stations that featured Guo were replaced by other programmes. Later, the Deyun Club announced that it would temporarily stop its performance schedule and conduct an internal rectification campaign (Peng 2010: 68).

Arguably, the CCP campaign may have begun in the first place because of the emergence of Guo Degang and like-minded peers who dared to bring attention to social malaises and taboos, challenging the official discourse and ideology. According to reporting from World Daily of America: 'the Beijing crosstalk performer Guo Degang became the "spotlight" of the Chinese media, however this Guo Degang incident is not a small problem confined to celebrities, but concerns the big and small *tuweizi* (土围子stubborn fortress of the harmful forces) that have emerged in the social transformation of China. The need to abolish these tuweizi is a new task facing China' (Peng 2010: 68). The critics and scholars of folk art also point out that Guo Degang's crosstalk performances lack upstanding values and cater to the lower classes, which leads only to 'simple' entertainment, providing the viewer with a 'stupid happiness' that has no humanistic concerns. If Guo keeps allowing this vulgar style to develop, it is argued, it will reduce the value of the Guo signature style of crosstalk performance (Yuan 2007: 164). The Beijing Folk Arts Association also published a Counter Three Vulgarities proposal to collaborate with the central government's appeal, expressing its determination to boycott coarseness, profanity and obscenity, and requesting that folk arts performers pay more attention to their moral cultivation and human quality (Peng 2010: 68). Just as the title of Peng Fei's article implies ('From Crosstalk Master to Representative of Three Vulgarities'), Guo Degang underwent a transformation from 'grassroots hero' to 'public enemy', which attests to the immense power wielded by the CCP dictatorship over potential challengers and opponents, and the regime's tight control of the entertainment world and of celebrities and stars. The Guo Degang case signifies the struggle between the newly emerging tuweizi – the unconformist, rebellious and critical social discourse – with the established, official and orthodox forces and regime – the struggle between the entertainment industry and mainstream propaganda and control. This struggle envisages an impending fight on the cultural stage of contemporary China, which perhaps will bring about new hope.

Following the case of Guo Degang, the crackdown on morally problematic and scandalous celebrities and stars continued in China, and escalated in 2018, when China's national Radio and Television Administration ordered the banishment of actors whose 'morality is not noble', who were 'tasteless, vulgar and obscene' or whose 'ideological level is low and have no class', and prescribed that 'actors with stains, scandals and problematic moral integrity' be banned (Seidel 2021). In the past decade, scandalous celebrity and stars have attracted enormous attention from media outlets and the Chinese public alike. Rather than public models and idols, they are more easily serving as representatives of social malaises, cultural debauchery and moral decadence. In 2014, internationally award-winning film director Wang Quanan (王全安) was arrested by the Beijing Dongcheng district police for soliciting prostitutes in his studio. In the same year, popular actor Huang Haibo (黄海波) was caught by the police for doing likewise. Huang remained in custody for fifteen days and received education in detention for six months. After the announcement of the punishment, Huang's company apologized to the public and Huang expressed that he would not lodge an appeal and did not wish any party or person to take this opportunity to create hype. He would unconditionally accept the punishment and regenerate himself. Several years later, in 2021, the so-called piano prince Li Yundi (李云迪) was arrested in Chaoyang district of Beijing for soliciting a prostitute. As a result, Li's appearance in a reality show was deleted and Li's membership in the Chinese Musicians' Association has been cancelled. The Chinese Association of Performing Arts has called for a boycott of Li Yundi to remind the performers and entertainers to strengthen self-discipline and enhance legal awareness.

It is widely known that selling sex and soliciting prostitutes were illegal in socialist China. Soon after the founding of the PRC, brothels were closed down by the CCP government and prostitutes were gathered in shelters to receive moral education and training in alternative occupations. However, in ancient and modern China, brothels have long been a constitutional part of the sociocultural life of Chinese people. Famous government officials, businessmen, writers and poets frequented brothels, and there were many famous and legendary prostitutes in Chinese history such as Li Shishi (李师师), Liu Rushi (柳如是) and

Dong Xiaowan (董小宛). In the Republican era, the lives of famous prostitutes such as Saijinhua (赛金花) and Xiaofengxian (小凤仙) were interwoven with the history of modern China. Saijinhua had been the concubine of a Qing Dynasty envoy to Europe and she had accompanied her husband to work and live in Europe so could speak fluent German. During the Eight-Nation Alliance invasion of Beijing towards the end of the Qing Dynasty, Saijinhua successfully persuaded German generals and soldiers not to implement indiscriminate killing and thereby protected the citizens of Beijing. Xiaofengxian is famous for her love story with the Republican-era patriotic general Cai E (蔡锷) and her support of Cai in his revolutionary career. Their story has been adapted into many contemporary Chinese films and TV drama serials.

Prostitutes' experiences and stories in ancient and modern China not only proved that their practice was legal; some of them even enjoyed high social status and recognition. However, in contemporary China, prostitutes are despised, isolated and judged as morally debauched and as violating human nature and social expectations. Particularly in the case of Huang Haibo, given he is single, his premarital sex could be easily understood and accepted by audiences. But in socialist China, a celebrity caught soliciting prostitutes will be subject to bans, moral judgement and legal punishment. It is of common knowledge that in mainland China, there operate different kinds of brothels under the guise of clubs, pubs, hair salons and pedicure shops that cater to various needs ranging from rich businessmen to Chinese people. These illegal brothels have normally built up connections with local police stations through bribery or they have supporters behind the scenes such as local government officials. Therefore, selling sex and soliciting prostitutes are not uncommon in China even though it is officially banned. However, when a celebrity's illegal dealings in sex are exposed, they are far more brittle given the damage that the revelations cause to their public image and career, and the financial loss that will inevitably ensue. Stars' popularity and influence among the public makes them a perfect conduit through which the government attempts to educate the public and consolidate its moral discipline and rule. Rumours and scandals revolving around celebrity figures occupy the headlines and prompt the public to explore and contemplate moral, gender and civil issues facing current Chinese society.

Scholars have noted that Chinese celebrity is 'a powerful instrument in the party state's discursive and symbolic repertoire, used to promote regime goals and solidify new governmentalities through signalling accepted modes of behaviour for mass emulation' (Sullivan & Kehoe 2018: 241–2). Celebrities' ability to influence considerable audiences and possibly impact society has rendered individual celebrities and the industry that produces and sponsors them 'subject to a system of control and instrumentalisation by the state' (Sullivan & Kehoe 2018: 241–2). China's celebrity industry is flourishing despite the harsh restrictions enforced by state and industry practitioners. Though celebrity culture in China can be fragile, it preserves a robust moral element (Sullivan & Kehoe 2018: 241–2). Scholars have also pointed out that the Chinese state has realized that popular devices including stars can spread political messages more efficiently than traditional propaganda can (Stockmann & Gallagher 2011: 459 cited in Sullivan & Kehoe 2018: 247), as 'Chinese audiences are accustomed to a diet of ideologically-driven "edutainment"' (Donald, Hong and Keane 2002; Wen 2013; Sullivan and Kehoe 2018: 243). According to the state's understanding of the propagation and political function of celebrities, it not only enlists scandalous celebrities as negative examples to convey their moral guidelines to the public; it also 'fabricate[s] celebrities as exemplars of model behaviours relating to consumption, "middle class" and "traditional" values, patriotism and acceptance of the political regime'. The state employs features of public relations, marketing and advertising to coin a hybrid 'pop-propaganda' system in order to promote state actors and state-sanctioned role models (Sullivan and Kehoe 2018: 252). However, even though celebrity or star figures are used to bolster the governing ideology of their age and are considered instrumental for the conservation of the hegemonic order, they have no control over their own images and the messages they carry to the public (Ribke 2015: 2).

The history of the construction of celebrities and stars in the PRC has had distinctive features in different historical and social contexts. In the early socialist stage, the party-state heavy-handedly manufactured propagandistic socialist models and idols for the Chinese people to imitate (Jeffreys 2012; Jeffreys and Edwards 2010). In the beginning of the Opening Up era, the evolution of the idol-making process witnessed the emergence of Western-style media-manufactured celebrities as idols of capitalist consumption (Jeffreys 2012). The evolution of the idol- and star-making process thus demonstrated the decline of socialist values and the rise of individualistic materialism, suggestive of a worsening account of Chinese popular culture and idol worship in the 1970s and 1980s. However, the CCP propaganda instruments have also progressed with the times and diversified and innovated China's celebrity-constructions, thereby maintaining the vitality of the socialist icons in commercial popular culture. In recent decades, the expansion of official propaganda that is embedded in popular culture products incorporates online documentaries, films, TV drama serials and education programmes, all of which are enlisted and co-opted by the state for propaganda goals. Illustrating how the CCP propaganda apparatus and tactics have evolved and become embedded in popular media products, contemporary Chinese popular media products bring to light the progression of the mainstream propaganda discourse in terms of its merging, cooperation and compromise with the commercial features of both the traditional and newly emerging entertainment media.

Among these innovations, a notable and unique element is how the propaganda apparatus creates socialist idols in inventive and engaging ways. Take *The Founding of a Republic* (建国大业) as a successful example. The film cleverly and innovatively enlists more than a hundred stars and celebrities, and it appears that their deployment as historical figures is the most viable method of ensuring that 'main-melody' discourse survives in a domain dominated by commercial elements. The internationally famed Chinese martial arts masters Jet Lee (李连杰) and Jackie Chan (成龙); Chinese super girl, Zhang Ziyi (章子怡); and the Hongkong film celebrities, Leung Kafai (梁家辉) and Andy Lau (刘德华), plus a group of A-list mainland young generation celebrities such as Chen Kun (陈坤) and Liu Ye (刘烨)[2] all play roles in *The Founding*, which makes the stars' brand power one of the most prominent features of the film. Many A-list stars only make an appearance in scenes such as where they are taking commemorative pictures at the first National Chinese People's Political Consultative Conference; however, they have fulfilled their duties as formative elements of a cultural celebratory carnival.

Another unique effect *The Founding* had on the commercialization of mainstream cultural propaganda is the introduction of humorous actors and stars such as Ge You (葛优) and Fan Wei (范伟)[3] into the cast, a move which lightens the solemn tone and serious themes of the film. Moreover, *The Founding* successfully created an intertextuality between historical figures and the film stars that enormously increased the curiosity and willingness of the mass audiences to view the film, shaping their expectations of a commercial mainstream movie. The unparalleled success of the film lies in its intelligent and inventive symmetry of the historical figures and the film stars in terms of their outer appearance, personality and mannerisms, which regenerate and renovate the historical figures on one hand and remodel the celebrities on the other.[4] According to Wang, the employment of such cultural ingredients – taking celebrities as an example – diminishes the vestige of political preaching and achieves a kind of 'political unconsciousness' (Wang 2009: 58). In summary, the win–win situation produced by the cooperation between mainstream blockbusters and celebrities enormously enhances the popularity of a film, hinting at a shift in the discourse of the mainstream propaganda.

While the government keeps producing state-endorsed celebrity in contemporary China, it continues to monitor and clamp down on those immoral behaviours of stars because the government understands that stars and celebrities provide a shortcut to disciplining and monitoring the Chinese people, particularly the young generations. Apart from trading in sex, engaging in extramarital affairs and keeping mistresses, there are other social malaises of present-day China, which are revealed in concentrated form through those degenerate stars. Extramarital affairs are still unacceptable and dishonourable in present-day China and were a common device employed by the party to denounce and criticize its cadres or any person in Maoist China.

Again taking Liu Xiaoqing as a typical example, she had an affair with a married actor, Chen Guojun (陈国军); Liu's real-life role as a 'third party' (第三者) could be regarded as unconventional and valiant because in the China of the 1980s people who 'interfered' in others' marriages could be sentenced to imprisonment, and this had already happened in the Chinese film circle (Liu 1995; Chen 1997). While maintaining a relationship with Chen Guojun, Liu Xiaoqing had other lovers, even after Chen divorced his first wife and married her. She had an affair with a co-star: Jiang Wen, an internationally famed actor-turned-director in China. Her behaviour was labelled *chugui* (出轨) by contemporary media reports, literally meaning 'off the rails', but in the contemporary Chinese popular lexicon is the term used to refer to the behaviour of a married man or woman who has an extramarital affair. Liu Xiaoqing's relationships with her lovers pushed the actress into the media spotlight but did not destroy her performing career.

Thirty years later, the emergence of professional paparazzi in mainland China has caused the exposure of many stars' extramarital affairs. In 2014, famous actor Wen Zhang's (文章) extramarital affair with actress Yao Di (姚笛)

was captured by China's number one paparazzi, Zhuo Wei (卓伟). Before Zhuo and his team released the evidence of Wen and Yao's affair, Wen and his broker contacted Zhuo to stop him with a large sum of money; however, Zhuo refused Wen's offer and insisted on publicizing his affair with Yao. It is pertinent to mention here the trend towards 'explosive revelation' in present-day Chinese entertainment and political spheres. In the entertainment world, the rise of professional and star paparazzi such as Zhuo Wei has made it harder for stars to maintain their perfect public image. In the political domain, the existence of exiled Chinese businessman Guo Wengui (郭文贵) and his regular revelation of explosive news about high-level Chinese officials has attracted enormous attention both in and outside China, which cultivated many loyal fans of Guo and turned him into a celebrity as well (as will be discussed in Chapter 4). Zhuo Wei's exposing of Wen Zhang and Yao Di's affair caused a devastating blow to Wen and Yao's careers and totally destroyed their public image as youth idols. Moreover, Wen and his wife Ma Yili's (马伊琍) marriage ended a couple of years after his affair with Yao was exposed.

Similar to Wen Zhang, famous middle-aged actor Wu Xiubo's (吴秀波) career has also been destroyed by revelations of his extramarital affair with a much younger female actress, Chen Yulin (陈昱霖). In 2018, Chen posted in her WeChat (微信) friend circle revealing her relationship with Wu, which had lasted for seven years. In 2019, Chen's parents published an open letter stating that after their daughter exposed her relationship with Wu in 2018, Wu and his broker and lawyer required Chen to withdraw her post on WeChat and clarify Wu's innocence in exchange for economic compensation. They reached an agreement and then Chen went abroad to take a rest. However, in late 2018, Wu asked Chen to come back to China and when Chen arrived at the Chinese airport she was arrested on grounds of violating Wu's privacy and extorting money from Wu. Wu's lawyer made an announcement saying the content of Chen's parents' open letter was not true and they had reported it to the public security bureau and would pursue legal action against Chen's parents. Later, Wu's wife released a statement saying they had been threatened and intimidated by Chen and were ordered to pay tens of millions of yuan, and after attempting to use persuasion and forbearance, they chose to report the matter to police.

After news of their scandal was released, netizens found Chen's Instagram account, which revealed that Chen had been living a luxurious lifestyle and used a private aeroplane to travel around the world. Wu later clarified that he had provided tens of millions of yuan to support Chen's plush life. In 2021, Chen was sentenced to three years in jail and handed a 100,000 yuan fine when she was found guilty of blackmailing and extorting money from Wu. This dramatic and chaotic fight between Wu and Chen not only illustrated the fraught relationship between men and women in China's entertainment world in particular; it also revealed the pragmatic and mercenary bonds between Chinese males and females in officialdom and the career field of present-day China. In the current Chinese social context where the CCP is tightening its moral control and rule that reminds people of Mao's era, scandalous celebrities like Wu and Chen serve as typical examples and were enlisted by the CCP to launch its moral campaign.

In 2021, Chinese-Canadian pop star Kris Wu (Wu Yifan 吴亦凡) was arrested on suspicion of rape. Police officers stated that the young star faced allegations of deceiving young women and forcing them to have sex with him. A nineteen-year-old female former fan of Wu, Du Meizhu (都美竹) exposed her story with Wu via social media platforms and accused Wu of luring and raping her in exchange for providing her job opportunities in the entertainment world. After his arrest, Wu declared his innocence and declared that he would pursue legal avenues against Du's claims. After Du came forward, more than twenty women also reported sexual harassment by Wu, which triggered the Chinese version of the MeToo movement in the entertainment domain. Wu's arrest has led to the bankruptcy of his public image. Many prestigious international brands terminated their contracts with Wu as a brand ambassador, and the Chinese government shut down his Weibo account. In 2022, Wu was sentenced to eleven years in prison and following his release he will be repatriated to Canada.

Observably, social media platforms such as Weibo and WeChat have played critical roles in Chinese people's social and civic life as they provide 'a medium for celebrities, opinion leaders, and grassroots users to express their views openly, freely, and at low cost' (Wang and Shi 2018: 518). Social media outlets such as Weibo are nurturing a new type of leadership and expanding its impact while undercutting the influence of state authorities (Lu and Qiu 2013).

Recently, there has been a trend in which ordinary netizens distribute original blog entries on numerous topics including reporting and commentary on current issues, women's rights, civil and political rights. The upsurge of citizen journalism and the thriving of user-generated content 'not only challenges the dominance of traditional media that is still heavily censored but also enriches grand narratives of traditional news reports by providing a more personalized perspective' (Guo 2016: 416).

These opinion leaders rally and direct public opinion and inspire large internet crowds to surround and watch social malpractice or injustice, and the creation of Weibo makes it simple for users to follow strangers such as celebrities, public figures and professionals, who would otherwise be out of reach in offline settings (You 2013; Wang and Shi 2018). Almost two decades ago, Sina.com created the term 'celebrity blogs' (*mingren boke*, 名人博客), which was the first portal website in China. The site quickly gathered together more than 2,500 celebrity bloggers by the end of 2005, which substantially boosted internet traffic on Sina.com by offering insider information that could effortlessly spawn millions of visits by fans, general readers and journalists. According to Guo (2016: 413–14), 'celebrity blogs effectively integrate the interests of celebrity bloggers (boost reputation), readers (voyeurism and star effects) and the website (generate profits), and exemplify online media companies' experimentation with new forms of communication and entertainment culture'.

In the case of Du Meizhu and Kris Wu, Du turned herself into an internet celebrity who advocates women's rights, which verifies that 'Celebrity is also one of the adhesives which, at a time when the realms of public politics, civil society, and private domestic life are increasingly fractured and enclosed in separate enclaves, serves to pull those separate entities together and to do its bit towards maintaining social cohesion and common values' (Inglis 2010: 3). Kris Wu's case indicates that the CCP government is determined to clean up the booming celebrity culture and fan culture in China's entertainment industry. According to Graeme Smith, 'the swiftness of Mr Wu's downfall after the allegations emerged suggested potential intervention by someone more powerful than the police', as he thinks 'this would have gone up to a very high decision-making level because it sends a very, very strong signal', and while the investigation work by the police is continuing, the state media has 'used the arrest to warn Mr Wu faces between 10 years and life in prison if convicted of serious offences'.

Apart from those degenerate celebrities and stars, there also exists an unhealthy fan culture that is full of distorted and morbid admiration of teenager and youth fans for their idols. No matter what their idols say and do, the young Chinese fans crazily follow and blindly admire, which in many cases has caused trouble to the fans in the areas of study, work and life. In the case of Wu, the discussion of his arrest and downfall has dominated Chinese social media platforms, and some of his loyal fans have even announced that they will bust Wu out of jail. The Chinese government has long been feeling discomfort with the chaotic and perverse fan culture of current China, which has taken advantage of the young fans and wasted their time and money. A new reality in contemporary China's entertainment scene is that the government cracks down on high-profile individuals because of its increasing belief that noxious celebrity culture is contaminating the minds of the country's youth (Zhang 2021).

Given this chaotic scenario and moral deterioration in the entertainment scene, together with its negative impact on Chinese audiences, Chinese censors are busy attempting to set things straight. State-controlled social media has been promoting messages including 'raise the threshold to become a celebrity', 'virtue before artistry' and 'the rewards of a moral society'. As Zhang (2021) notes, 'A key issue is that the Chinese government sees celebrities as not just entertainers, but also as role models for the general public and there is no room for mistakes or for causing any sort of bad influence.' Therefore, public figures should set an example and it is reasonable that they should pay a higher price for their mistakes. In China, public figures including celebrities and stars shoulder more social responsibility. The wisdom holds that they should be extremely careful because if they become morally problematic or commit crimes it will cause huge impact and harm on society and will lead the value orientation of the teenagers and the youths astray. However, scholars hold a different opinion towards the government's conception of celebrity figures and point out that 'members of the public should understand that celebrities are ordinary people and not moral exemplars, even though their domestic and international standing as representatives of China requires them to conduct themselves as perfectly as possible' (Jeffreys 2011: 9). Accordingly, the public should not develop disillusionment towards scandalous celebrities and stars as they should not have unrealistically high expectation of their idols.

The case of Kris Wu has generated discussion regarding another sensitive issue: the nationality of celebrities and stars. Many Chinese celebrities and stars have taken foreign citizenship or were born in a foreign country. Their foreign nationality is often criticized or mocked by Chinese netizens as evidence of their disloyalty to China. In the 2022 Winter Olympic Games held in Beijing, the young athlete Gu Ailing (Eileen Gu 谷爱凌), who possesses both American and Chinese nationality, represented China and won many medals, putting her in the spotlight of Chinese media outlets that hailed her as a Chinese national hero full of patriotic sentiment. Taking Kris Wu's case as a typical example, the Chinese state media tried to attract attention to his nationality. In the wake of Wu's arrest, the state-run media outlets have sought to send a message: neither fame nor a foreign passport will help you avoid Chinese justice. The *Legal Daily* (法制日报), a publication of the central government, comments that Mr Wu's arrest teaches society a very tangible lesson: that everyone is equal before the law (吴亦凡们不能只讲名利不知敬畏, 2021). Moreover, *People's Daily* (人民日报), the Communist Party's mouthpiece, used the arrest of Wu to caution that foreign citizenship was not any protection against violating Chinese laws, a message amplified by other state media including CCTV, which made it clear that no one has any immunity. Star aura is no protection, fans are no protection and nor are foreign passports. No one has the privilege of violating the law (人民日报评吴亦凡被刑拘: 法律面前没有顶流, 2021).

Scandalous celebrities and stars have become a key conduit through which topical and controversial social malaises and problems are analysed and debated. In 2021, popular actress Zheng Shuang's (郑爽) former partner accused her of deserting two surrogate children in the United States. Zheng then disappeared from public vision for several months, which almost ended her career. She had also been caught evading tax in 2019. Zheng is a young generation Chinese pop star who is famous for her rebellious behaviour. As noted by Pollock, Mishina and Seo (2016: 235), when viewed positively, those 'deviant' or non-conforming behaviours create a 'rebel' celebrity persona attractive to some sponsors; on the other hand, if the celebrity's intractable conduct is considered undesirable it can lead to an 'outlaw' image that causes a loss of celebrity and potentially increases infamy. Undoubtedly in Zheng's case, her 'outlaw' status has resulted in her loss of favour from both the government and her fans.

In 2013, the internationally famed and awarded Chinese Fifth Generation film director Zhang Yimou was reported to have fathered three children with a young dancer who was more than thirty years younger than him. This scandal triggered hot social debate over China's One Child Policy, its legal scaffolding and the privileges enjoyed by celebrities and famous and powerful people of present-day China. The couple was reported to have married in 2011, meaning that their three children were born out of wedlock, and according to China's population and family planning law, they had exceeded the quota that only allowed one couple to have one child. In 2013, Zhang and his wife apologized to the public, and they paid a 7.48 million yuan fine in 2014. China's One Child Policy was implemented from the early 1980s and was suspended in 2015, since which time a couple has been allowed to have two or more children.

Chinese people, particularly those urban workers who were affiliated with a socialist work unit in the 1980s and 1990s, were doomed to be dismissed by their work unit if they choose to exceed the birth quota. Zhang's case generated hot discussion among the Chinese public as they felt it unfair that celebrities and stars like Zhang could enjoy the privilege of giving birth to more children at the expense of just paying a sum of money (which, while an astronomical figure for most salary earners, was more than affordable for the Zhang couple). Thus, many Chinese people felt it unfair that rich and famous people have privileges and enjoy a superior social and legal status than themselves, which indicates the unequal and unfair nature of the current Chinese social and legal systems. It is widely agreed across China that there exist privileged social classes including the 'rich second generation' (富二代), 'the official second generation' (官二代) and 'the star second generation' (星二代), and the enormous wealth, political and social resources and connections these privileged social strata possess and monopolize have led to the unequal social reality, social malaises and corruption of present-day China. The Zhang Yimou scandal spurred the public's attention and interest to question the unfairness of the current social reality in China, and furthermore, to explore and criticize the civil and sociopolitical practices that allow the survival of the privileged social groups. Zhang's case proves that scandalous celebrity in China is held to account for its usefulness amidst the continuing negotiation of society's demands, worries, disputes and flaws. The making of an affect-driven intimate public demonstrates not only celebrity power but also its function as a catalyst for debates over social issues and civic rights.

Celebrity public intellectuals and matters of public concern

There has been a culture of celebrity activism in America that continues to the present day. Celebrities and stars have participated in wartime and presidential campaigns since the inception of Hollywood. Some high-profile celebrities devoted themselves to civil rights movements, using their public image and media networks to bring attention to and shape those debates (Emilie 2015: 243). Some scholars point out that 'celebrities draw the power and influence of their personal brand appeal and can transform society'; particularly in recent years, 'this form of activism has further been facilitated by social media and microblogging platforms, like Twitter, where they enjoy the mass appeal and the freedom to communicate their un-inhibited opinions' (Jain, Sharma and Behl 2021: 1–2).

At the international level, the then UN secretary general Kofi Annan acted as the prime mover in 1997 to give particular boost to the United Nations' (UN) courtship of celebrity. Annan 'decided to use writers, actors, singers and sportsmen extensively in order to persuade reluctant governments to honour their pledges made in UN forums and to inspire international public opinion to support UN causes' (Alleyne 2008 cited in Huliaras and Tzifakis 2010: 259). In 1997, the UN created a privileged set of celebrities including George Clooney and Michael Douglas who were called 'Messengers of Peace' to 'help focus global attention on the noble aims of the UN'. As Huliaras and Tzifakis pointed out, 'the use of celebrities by the United Nations has proved particularly effective both in raising public awareness and in fundraising for the organisation's agencies' (Huliaras and Tzifakis 2010: 260).

Given celebrity's ability to enter into various realms of public life ranging from politics to culture in Western liberal democracies as a 'mobile insurgent'

(Nayar 2021: 6), many scholars argue that the growth of celebrity politics 'undermines democratic governance by trivializing politics and turning it into "theatre"' (Jeffreys 2016: 59). Others argue that celebrity spectacles impede the democratic process by diverting citizens from important issues of contention (Fletcher 2015: 467), which is 'fundamentally depoliticizing' (Kapoor 2012: 1), and they argue against the 'commodification of politics at the hands of celebrities' (Street 2004; Gies 2009; Kellner 2010; Wheeler 2013; Nayar 2021). In contrast, some scholars suggest that celebrity activism may 'act as a potential check on executive power, and engage people in politics who might not otherwise be interested' (Jeffreys 2016: 59). Moreover, some scholars note that most celebrity activists today manage to stay away from the most provocative domestic or international political issues lest political disputes jeopardize their careers (Huliaras and Tzifakis 2010: 262).

No matter what concerns are raised in Western societies about celebrity activism, no one can deny the appeal and influence of celebrity in the social, cultural and political domains in these Western democracies. In comparison, the situation in the PRC, which is an established authoritarian superpower, is different. As Jeffreys notes: 'China's private entrepreneurs and celebrities do not comprise an established "power elite" as in Western societies, that is, a networked group of non-elected, "non-state" actors who influence national and increasingly international government decision-making' (2016: 765).

In present-day China, celebrity implies a broad range of famous and accomplished individuals in various professions and domains including film and TV stars, crosstalk performers, celebrity hosts, journalists and writers. In ancient China, performers or entertainers were discussed with derogatory undertones. There was discrimination and disrespect for actors and actresses from the noble and upper social classes and lower social cohorts alike because performers rarely received education or had the opportunity to participate in civil and political affairs; instead, their main social function was to provide recreation and entertainment for other social classes.

During the Republican era, left-wing writers and actors joined the revolutionary cause and contributed to the awakening of Chinese people's patriotic and nationalist enthusiasm through their performance and artistic creations. This lifted the social and political status of performers to revered artists who personified national and patriotic passions.

During the Anti-Japanese War, several famous Chinese Peking Opera masters such as Mei Lanfang (梅兰芳) and Cheng Yanqiu (程砚秋) refused to perform for the Japanese captains and soldiers in order to awaken Chinese people's national spirit to resist the Japanese invasion. From – and in fact before – 1949, performers and artists advanced their professional careers under the instructions of the party and became 'people's artists', devoting themselves to spreading the party policy and lines. Nevertheless, some were persecuted and purged at the height of incessant political movements and struggles such as the Cultural Revolution. This socialist use of celebrities as moral actors and state policy advocates shows the incorporation of celebrity into the CCP apparatus, which demonstrates that 'celebrities can be both modern and popular figures yet embedded in the state's agenda and interests' (Hood 2015: 416). During the Opening Up era, under a relatively open and tolerant social and political atmosphere, actors and performers acquired celebrity and star status as an effective entertainment industry emerged and developed in China.

In Western societies, celebrities fulfil the role of public intellectuals and social and cultural activists in many political, social and public welfare discussions and campaigns. As one commentator frames it, they are engaged in 'celebrity activism' (Marshall 2014: xxiii–xxiv). As noted by Huliaras and Tzifakis, in recent years, celebrities have taken a keen interest in world politics and many of them have become well-recognized global activists (Huliaras and Tzifakis 2010: 255–6). Celebrity activism is argued to be largely an Anglo-Saxon and Black American celebrity phenomenon. In modern-day China, none of the motions raised by celebrity delegates at the 11th National People's Congress (NPC) resulted in policy change even though numerous celebrities 'are frequently called upon to express their views on and lend their support to all manner of weighty social issues' (Fletcher 2015: 458). According to Jeffreys, 'China's celebrity politicians might be more appropriately termed "celebrity party-supporters"' (Jeffrey 2016: 64). Moreover, the failure of these celebrities to contribute to policy change shows that 'media coverage of their political involvement has not accorded them the social authority that makes celebrity politics such a controversial feature of Western liberal democracies' (Jeffreys 2016: 69).

Though there has not yet formed a distinctive or notable Chinese celebrity activism spectacle in present-day China, in recent decades, a similar political and sociocultural role has been fulfilled by contemporary Chinese celebrities. As noted by David Marshall (2014: xi):

> In our contemporary world, the instantaneity of celebrity images and the ubiquity of our 'search' culture mean that celebrity inhabit a social space closer to us than ever before. Thus, taking their intimate relationship with the general public, and particularly with their fans, celebrity and stars can easily turn themselves into 'celebrity activists'.

China has its own cohort of 'celebrity activists'. Some scholars point out that Chinese celebrity commitment in public health promotion and humanitarian undertaking is an immensely active and rapidly developing arena. In the last decade, Chinese celebrities have taken up the cause of welfare services such as health advocacy, housing and education support (Hood 2015: 414). For example, Chinese actors Pu Cunxi (b. 1953, 濮存昕) and Jiang Wenli (b. 1969, 蒋雯丽) play a significant role in promoting AIDS prevention activities. Both have served as 'AIDS ambassadors' in China for many years and both enjoy immense popularity and respect among Chinese audiences. The roles Jiang Wenli and Pu Cunxi played in their previous TV and film works were model representatives of the traditional merits of Chinese men and women such as gentle, capable, virtuous, wise, civil and courteous. Turner argues that stardom is 'a form of public personality with whom [the public] identify, in whom they invest and maintain a personal interest, and to whom is ascribed a value that is cultural or social rather than merely economic' (2004: 14). Marshall remarks that '[c]elebrity status also confers on the person a certain discursive power: within society, the celebrity is a voice above others, a voice that is channelled into the media systems as being legitimately significant' (1997: x). Compared with that in Western societies, this discursive power possessed by Chinese celebrity and stars is often under surveillance, discipline and even manipulation of the state propaganda machines as the CCP government tries to control the speech and conduct of influential public figures and will ban them if their viewpoints and deeds do not align with state propaganda and policy. Without state support and endorsement, celebrity humanitarianism may not have become fashionable (Hood 2015: 421).

Other scholars examine celebrity involvement in the NPC and the Chinese People's Political Consultative Conference. For example, as Jeffreys (2016: 58) found:

Celebrity participation in these forums shows that celebrity politics in China chiefly functions to support government policies, but also reveals a broadening of elite networks and the capacity of those networks to generate public discussion of alternative policies and politics. Rather than supporting claims that celebrity politics is spectacular or theatrical, it demonstrates instead the connections between celebrity and mundane aspects of Chinese governance.

Xi Jinping's wife, Peng Liyuan (彭丽媛), is typical of those celebrities who are public policy followers and supporters. As a prominent singer in mainland China, Peng uses her unique public profile as both a star and First Lady, and 'has developed a strong relationship to the Chinese public increasingly defined on trust and hope, in an apolitical and highly gendered consciousness', which 'signals the beginning of a new technique to maintain power and international and local credibility amidst a crisis of legitimacy at home' as 'increasing trust in celebrities remakes their social role and political function' (Hood 2015: 423).

Those celebrities who take up the role of social and cultural activism in present-day China generate public discussion of alternative policies and controversial social and cultural events. While the realm of celebrity is subject to restraint and regulation, individual celebrities have used the affordances of their status to raise public consciousness around LGBT issues, concepts of Chineseness and filiality and severe environment pollution caused by unscrupulous development of the economy (Sullivan and Kehoe 2018: 246). In contemporary societies, celebrities may be employed to galvanize support for adjustments to government rules on the health, youth, the environment and multiculturalism (Cashmore 2006; Turner 2004; Jeffreys and Edwards 2010). Because of advances in technology and media know-how, celebrities are capable of affecting and shaping matters of public appeal in contemporary society (Hood 2010). In other words, they have the ability to expand their influence beyond its traditional realm and are vigorously involved in doing their part for humanity by using their reputation for the benefit of the broader community. Celebrities can rally massive global audiences to the particular causes they support, and by boosting publicity and capital they can even inspire government and organizations' politics and practices. The celebrity's agency has become a crucial venue of a public voice of power and influence (Marshall 2014).

In current China, many celebrities have started using their fame and stardom to attract attention to controversial social stigmas and problems. The female celebrity TV host and journalist Chai Jing's (柴静, b. 1976) participation in the reporting of the 2003 SARS outbreak in Beijing not only won her trust and respect among the general public of China but also elevated her to the status of celebrity host. In early 2015, Chai made a fiercely debated documentary titled *Under the Dome* (穹顶之下), which examined smog pollution in Beijing. On the mainland, the documentary was banned just a week after its release for its 'negative impact' on the general public, who doubted the capacity of the government to solve the smog problem. In the documentary, Chai Jing interviews government officials to ascertain the reasons behind these high levels of air pollution. Consequently, the conclusion of the documentary points to the government as the main factor behind the heavy smog pollution. The desperate pursuit of economic growth engineered by a state with a developmental approach together with a lack of relevant laws to regulate the discharge of industrial waste are two key elements identified in the documentary. Chai Jing's social influence as an established, respectful and celebrity reporter contributed to the sensational social effect of *Under the Dome*. Later in March 2015, the Chinese minister of environmental protection Chen Jining (陈吉宁) said in a media conference that he had watched Chai's documentary and had sent her a text message to express his gratitude to her. Chen said, 'Chai's documentary is admirable as it awakens the public's environmental consciousness. Chai's investigation and reporting should be encouraged, and the government will adopt and implement the media's advice' (环保部长: 我完整看了 '穹顶之下' 柴静没给我增加压力, 2015).

The chief editor of CCTV's signature investigative journalism programme, *Focus Report* (焦点访谈), commented on Chai's action as 'civil investigation in the era of the internet'. Zhuang Yongzhi (庄永志) said:

As far as I am aware, this is the most authoritative investigation on smog pollution with the broadest perspective that utilised the richest tools and methods . . . which will trigger a new round of actions to control the smog, ranging from improvement of legislative to the adjustment of public policy and to the personal duty of individual citizens . . . Chai, as an individual and independent citizen rather than organisational employee or government official, was able to research the harm caused by smog pollution and the strategic plan and the stipulation and implementation of energy policy. She could evaluate the gains and losses of these methods and actions from a perspective of information disclosure and democratic decision-making. Netizens could view the documentary with trust and admiration of the personal charisma of the producer and out of their concern about their own interest and benefit and their attention to and participation in civil events.

Under the Dome also attracted attention from celebrity activists including Cui Yongyuan (崔永元), Yao Chen (姚晨) and Yuan Li (袁立), who expressed their admiration and respect for Chai Jing. Similarly, the documentary elicited enthusiastic responses from the netizens because it provided them with a shortcut to understand the harm of the smog pollution, particularly its long-term impact on the life of future generations. Further, after viewing the documentary, many netizens expressed the opinion that only knowing the harm of the smog pollution was not enough; they had to take action to control and stop it. Herein lies the greatest achievement of Chai's documentary: it mobilized various powers on social media platforms and attracted the attention of tens of millions of Chinese citizens to the issue of smog pollution

Similar to Chai Jing, contemporary Chinese celebrities and stars have spoken up for the general public and disadvantaged groups. In their performances, TV or film works, social media posts and interviews, they draw attention to and report on the 'underground' and shadowy China rather than the thriving official imagery of China's radical economic transition and social reconfiguration, thereby revealing a poignant, non-mainstream rendition of the social hardships encountered by Chinese people. It is widely known that the rapid and unscrupulous economic great leap forward of China in the past forty-five years has led to rampant corruption, an ever-widening income gap and generated disadvantaged social cohorts. Demolition, laid-off workers, disillusioned youths and those marginalized social groups are the most frequent thematic foci and topics of China's investigative journalists and independent documentary and film-makers. For example, China's internationally famed sixth-generation director Jia Zhangke (贾樟柯) has been labelled a 'cinematic migrant worker' (电影民工) (Braester 2010: 301 cited in Wagner 2013: 364) because his films employ a bleak and candid cinematic language and his photography and stories probe into the social unrest and the mental anxiety and the perplexity that permeate Chinese society. Jia's family belongs to the salary-earning social stratum that has an adverse interpretation of China's nouveau rich and its privileged social tiers. It is possibly because of his family background that Jia's films speak out for China's common folks and their struggles in a society underpinned by escalating financial inequality and social bigotry. Starting with his hometown trilogy *Xiao Wu* (小武, 1997), *Platform* (站台, 2000) and *Unknown Pleasures* (任逍遥, 2002), Jia outlines the precipitous change that occurred in the economic and sociocultural domains during the initial two decades after the implementation of the opening-up policy. His work is centred on a county located in a backward inland city of Shanxi Province, where Jia spent his childhood and teenage days. The attrition and disbanding of the economic, emotional and ethical bonds between individuals and state-run work units, between friends, family members and lovers, exhibit paradoxes and idiosyncrasies that are entrenched in China's hasty social makeover.

In an interview conducted with Jia Zhangke, he sharply pointed out the morbid culture of modern-day China's film market, which is dominated by so-called main melody films (主旋律电影) that promote party propaganda and policy. Jia expressed his concerns about the 'abnormal' situation of China's film industry and openly questioned the motives and goals of the party propaganda apparatus (Jia Zhangke: Buneng ba zhongguo dianying 2022). Jia Zhangke's comments and his film works make him a public activist in contemporary China, who articulates the voice of the Chinese people and the disadvantaged social cohorts.

Similar to Jia Zhangke, Guo Degang (郭德纲), the contemporary crosstalk (*xiangsheng* 相声) master, also poignantly and astutely identifies the social malaises of contemporary China in his folk arts performances. In sharp contrast to officially sanctioned topics, Guo's works revolve around sensitive and controversial social issues and problems (Fan 2006: 87; Yuan 2007: 164; Xiang 2008: 156; Liu 2010: 75–6). These sensitive social topics include the ruthless competition in the employment market, growing unemployment, social discrimination towards peasant workers, unspoken rules in the entertainment industry, mistresses of the wealthy, gang violence, prostitution and pornography, which have aroused growing discontent and indignation among Chinese people.

On crosstalk's role in criticizing the Cultural Revolution after the overthrow of the Gang of Four, Link (1984: 84) comments: 'it is *xiangsheng* above everything else that people say, "vents one's gall" (*jiehen* 解恨).' Link's comment reveals why Guo Degang and his performances are so popular among the

Chinese people and why he is regarded as a culture hero. Guo's crosstalk allows people to let off steam, especially those Chinese who have long suffered from the rampant social injustice, official corruption and the widening gap between the rich and the poor. In his performances, Guo specifically ferrets out the injustice in Chinese society. Thus, his crosstalk works act as counter-rhetoric to the official propaganda, which sings the praises of the CCP government. This has landed him in trouble and incurred regular bans of his performances.

Both Jia Zhangke and Guo Degang are scandal-free celebrities. Not only is the quality of their films and performances high; they have also won respect from the public as grassroots cultural heroes who have fulfilled the role of a public intellectual. Compared with Guo and Jia, who were born in the 1970s, a younger-generation opinion leader is celebrity writer and director Han Han (韩寒), who was born in the 1980s. As one of China's best-known writers and bloggers, Han Han uses his blog to comment on and to unmask the social maladies and problems within the political and sociocultural settings of today's China. His writing mixes amusing observations, jokes, quips, oblique caricatures and the sexualization of politics. It blurs blazing satire and chilling sarcasm with joyous laughter and furious swearing, generating a much sought-after and enjoyable relief for his readers. Han Han has been seen as a defiant youth, a genuine citizen and a mentor of public opinion, and his work and his values have been examined and assessed accordingly. Once seen as a playful youth by some conservative and mainstream critics, Han Han is now judged by some social and cultural agencies as a humanist, and one of China's most influential public intellectuals. Through the advanced media outlet that he created by blogging, Han Han finds his market niche and presents a nicely wrapped cultural product to his fans. Unlike those students and intellectual leaders of the 4th June Tiananmen demonstration who fought at the forefront to initiate conversation and negotiation with the party officials in order to promote democracy and the anti-corruption campaign, and unlike Liu Xiaobo (刘晓波) who died in prison for his promotion of 'Charter 08' (零八宪章), Han Han enjoys his multiple forms of stardom as a writer and a director, voicing his concerns about his country through innovative and popular media platforms of blogging.

Undoubtedly, Han Han performs extremely well in fashioning an unconventional and charismatic public image for himself, which is celebrity-cum-intellectual. The 'Han Han phenomenon' has drawn vast attention from the critics and the Chinese people alike, and his capacity in acting as the 'fourth estate', which provides critique of the Chinese government, has been applauded and admired. While his blogs are very popular and influential, he himself has perceived that his 'influence and power' as a public intellectual is not sufficient to affect the actions of the government. However, at least, Han Han and his blog postings provide a venue for the Chinese people to vent their frustrations regarding their sufferings in the corrupt, unfair and chaotic social reality of today's China.

In recent years, another celebrity host, Cui Yongyuan, has stood out in the entertainment world to reveal the social and legal corruption of current China. Cui has become widely known and popular among the Chinese public for his outspoken nature and his conscientiousness and responsibility as a public figure. *Tell It Like It Is* (实话实说) is the talk show programme broadcast on CCTV from which Cui emerged and gained popularity. In this programme, Cui insisted on focusing on controversial social topics and issues. He endeavoured to trigger genuine and effective public discussion that might be considered by the government as sensitive and harmful to the maintaining of a harmonious society and the legitimacy of the party's rule. Therefore, Cui suffered from long-term depression and finally decided to resign from CCTV as he knew there was no freedom of speech on the state-run and state-controlled media platforms. In 2018, Cui revealed A-list Chinese female actress Fan Bingbing's (范冰冰) illegal conduct of signing fake performance contracts to avoid paying huge amounts of tax, which shocked the Chinese public and triggered challenges from the disadvantaged groups to the privileged social cohorts. In the same year, Cui exposed corruption within the Supreme Court of China, and under huge media and public pressure, the CCP's Political and Legislative Affairs Committee (中共中央政法委) launched investigations and clarified that one of the judges of the Supreme Court had been involved in illegal acts while on duty. In 2020, Cui continued his 'whistle blower movement' and exposed via his YouTube account that there indeed existed a phenomenon of paid test-takers in the university entrance exam in Shandong Province. In the YouTube video, Cui directly labelled the former chief editor of *Global Times* newspaper (环球时报, a mouthpiece for the CCP government), Hu Xijin (胡锡进), an 'ass licker' and emphasized that the outcome announced by the government's investigation group regarding the paid test-takers should not be trusted. Cui's 'whistle blower movement' made him a courageous public activist and celebrity in the eyes of the Chinese people. Many of them worried about Cui's safety and some of them even wondered whether Cui was still alive. In 2020, Cui's studio announced through the foreign media channels of Twitter and YouTube that Cui had been hospitalized, and since then there has rarely been any news about Cui's situation released in or outside of China (崔永元近况受瞩 参股公司及法人被限制消费, 2021). Cui's former CCTV colleague Bai Yansong (白岩松), another celebrity investigative reporter and TV host, has praised Cui thus: 'Cui Yongyuan is like a soldier who fights the illegal behaviours and activities in Chinese society ceaselessly. Even though his power is limited, at least people knows that righteousness still exists' (崔永元还活着吗央视对他的态度是可定的, 2021). According to Guo (2016: 416), 'Han Han and Cui Yongyuan have not only directed netizens' attention to various controversial issues, but also bolstered societal interest in debating public intellectuals' role in an authoritarian regime' (Guo 2016: 416).

After the news of Cui Yongyuan's hospitalization was released, his friends were praying for him, including famous actress Yuan Li. In the past two decades, Yuan has joined those celebrity public activists to voice her concerns about the social inequality and problems of current China. Back in 2003, Yuan's conscientiousness and sense of responsibility as a public figure were evident in her active participation in the fights against the SARS pandemic. In 2008 after the Wenchuan earthquake in Sichuan Province, Yuan donated 310,000 yuan to the victims of that disaster. In 2015, Yuan became a volunteer to help pneumoconiosis patients. Pneumoconiosis is a deadly occupational disease that afflicts miners. It became a sensitive social topic because there are so many illegal coal mines in China that do not provide basic job security to the miners and exploit them terribly. There is a widely spread rumour circulating on the Chinese internet that some illegal coal mines are like private prisons; some miners have been abducted and live and work like criminals with no or very little pay, and they could be killed if they try to escape.

Another factor that contributes to the sensitivity of the pneumoconiosis issue is the lack of public and free medical treatment and services to those patients who develop this illness, and this has led to many of them dying in a state of extreme suffering. The rare coverage by state-run media outlets of the pneumoconiosis patients' miserable conditions led to the Chinese public's lack of awareness of their tragic circumstances. In this sense, as a public figure and activist, Yuan Li's exposé of the suffering and dismal circumstance of those patients won her regard and esteem not only from her fans but also from the general public. Yuan was ranked among the top Chinese celebrities in terms of charity work performed in 2015 and 2017. In 2019, Yuan posted the receipts of her charity donations, which showed she had donated 400,000 yuan over a three months' period. Yuan has expressed that she will devote her whole life to help those pneumoconiosis victims. Undoubtedly, Yuan Li has joined Cui Yongyuan in the 'whistle blower movement'.

Owing to her outspoken personality and her conscientiousness as a public figure and activist, Yuan Li's blog account has been permanently banned, and she feels confused about this disastrous outcome. In the case of Yuan Li and Cui Yongyuan, it is not difficult to discern that in today's China, to be a conscientious and responsible celebrity and public activist one has to pay a huge price. The cost could be the end of one's professional career, massive financial loss and even psychological torment and suffering. Thus, those celebrities, including TV and film stars, famous presenters, athletes, journalists and writers who have the courage to speak up for the Chinese people and to openly discuss controversial and sensitive issues, deserve applause and respect. It is they who shoulder the responsibility and fulfill the function of a true public intellectual, using their popularity and appeal to rouse the Chinese people and to inspire them to think independently and critically.

In the most recent Ukraine War launched by Russian's president Putin and his followers, the CCP propaganda machines employed the exact rhetoric and tone of the Russian state-run media when reporting the nature of the Ukraine War (俄媒移花接木抹黑乌军抢劫, 中国媒体学舌, 2022). That is, the war arose from the pressure of NATO and the America-led suppression and sanction of Russia, rather than Russia's invasion of a sovereign nation. In Russia, Putin has stipulated new laws that could be used to punish those Russian people who spread anti-war information and question the rationale of the Ukraine War, and Russia's state-controlled media unanimously acclaimed Putin's decision in starting the war. Independent media almost disappeared in Russia and anti-war protesters and demonstrators have been arrested and could be sentenced to jail. It is widely known that in current China under the reign of the CCP, the state propaganda machine monitors and issues directives to not only state-run media outlets but also commercial media and social media platforms on how to report on civil and international issues, and what topics and themes are sensitive and taboo.

In the case of the Ukraine War, given that China's political stance is on the side of Russia, political leaders even ignore the treaty signed between China and Ukraine regarding protecting and guaranteeing each other's safety and sovereignty. This, of course, will cause trouble for China as well. Since Russia has recognized the independence of the two areas of Ukraine, Donetsk and Luhansk, should other countries recognize the independence of the Xinjiang Uyghur and Tibet Autonomous Regions if they announced their independent status? Another focus of the Ukraine War is that it has caused numerous civilian casualties; this goes against the will of any person who loves peace and respects basic human rights. The Chinese government's silence on Russia's invasion is contributing to civilian casualties in Ukraine. Thus, some honest and responsible Chinese celebrities and stars have expressed their anti-war attitude and condemned Putin's starting the Ukraine War in the era of peace. On 1 March 2022, famous Chinese transgender TV host Jin Xing (金星) published a post on her blog mentioning the Chained Woman issue and articulated her anti-Putin and anti-Ukraine War viewpoint. Jin's original post read as follows:

> The most horrible thing in 2022 is: a woman who is chained by her neck says, 'this world has deserted me!' A crazy Russian man says, 'if I am not allowed to continue to be the president, I will desert the world!' . . . stop the war and pray for peace!

Right after Jin posted her words on her blog platform, this blog entry was censored and Jin explained that she herself did not delete this post. Later, Jin was banned from posting on her blog platform. It is worth mentioning that Jin is a very influential figure in Chinese entertainment circles not only because of her transgender identity but also because of her outspokenness and frank personality. Jin has 13.5 million fans on her blog channel, so her anti-Ukraine War viewpoints had the potential to reach many Chinese people who had been brainwashed by the government propaganda on the Ukraine War. As Soukup notes, 'fans amplify and modify a sort of "iconic identification" with celebrities, especially in terms of individuals' identities, self-expressions, and political discourse' (Soukup 2006: 333). Jin Xing insisted on her anti-war appeal to the Chinese people and quoted philosopher Hannah Arendt's classic words in her blog poster to awaken Chinese people's ability to think critically and independently:

When a man refuses to think, he surrenders his uniquely human qualities, and is unable to make moral judgments any longer. This kind of incompetence in thinking has caused many ordinary people to commit appalling crimes. When ordinary people give up thinking completely, then catastrophe is not far away. (中国女星曾因'反战'遭围剿！不惧网暴再度喊话 2022)

Jin Xing fulfills her duty as a public activist because as an opinion leader she 'challenges the information monopoly and direct[s] public opinion' (Lu and Qiu 2013 cited in Wang and Shi 2018: 519). In contemporary China, this group of public activists consists of social and cultural elites with high social prestige and good character who represent voices of diverse social factions. Jin Xing is also an opinion leader who voices her opinion through her blog, which 'functions as an online school of civic and political participation to foster political interest and civic virtue among Chinese people'. Further, Wang and Shi's research shows that 'closely following opinion leaders' blog significantly increases Chinese college students' political interests and civic virtue, both of which are important antecedents of online expressive participation' (Wang and Shi 2018: 528).

It is shocking and disappointing to realize that in China there are many people who have shown their support of Putin and his invasion of Ukraine. There are a couple of causes that have led to this mindset. First, the CCP's propaganda and 'thought work' concerning America's hegemony in the current global environment has had some effect on the Chinese people, who think that Putin's courage in resisting American domination showed guts. He won respect from the Chinese people, who think him a hero representing nations that are under America's suppression and sanction. Since the founding of the PRC, the CCP has viewed America as the number one enemy of China because of ideological differences and economic road lines. Though the Sino-American relationship thawed in the 1970s owing to mutual interest in containing the Soviet Union, and the relationship between the two countries indeed experienced a honeymoon period between the 1980s and the early 2000s, the most recent American presidents' 'Pivot to Asia' strategy has laid bare the competitive and even hostile relationship between China and America in recent decades. America's punishment of the Chinese technological juggernaut Huawei and the trade wars between the two countries, the investigation of the origin of the Covid epidemic and the issues of Taiwan and Hong Kong have seen the Sino-American relationship deteriorate at an unprecedented speed.

Further, China's 'wolf warrior' diplomatic strategy has also contributed to the antagonistic bond between China and America. Therefore, a Cold War logic has been revitalized in the mindset of Chinese citizens, who see America as China's enemy and whoever stands up to America as China's ally and friends.

Second, similar to the Russian people, who have long been immersed in and intoxicated by the ancient glories of their nation, Chinese people also harbour a 'Chinese dream', which is to revive the Chinese nation to its past prestige and prosperity. Some Chinese people embrace a strong nationalistic sentiment, considering the suffering and bullying encountered by modern and contemporary China to be a humiliation and shame that are unacceptable. This has triggered a vengeful sentiment among the Chinese people. There exists a discourse of popular nationalism that is driven by a sentiment of victimization held by contemporary Chinese. The causes of this mental trauma, which has been acquired over the past one hundred years or so, were the invasions and humiliations at the hands of imperialist forces from the West and Japan, as is clearly demonstrated in the *China Can Say No* (中国可以说不) book series by popular nationalist author Song Qiang (宋强). This resentment was consolidated by the American bombing of the Chinese embassy in Belgrade in 1999, which triggered large-scale street demonstrations against the US government and motivated cyber-nationalists to hack into the US embassy's website in Beijing. Similar protests followed the downing of an American spy plane off the coast of Southern China in 2001 and the boycott of the 2008 Beijing Olympics torch relay, marking the peak of the popular nationalist campaigns. The victimization narrative first emerged in the mid-1990s from the grassroots and was later appropriated by the CCP to serve its nationalist propaganda. The aforementioned sentiment of anti-America hegemony, the sense of victimization and a vengeful mindset have contributed to Chinese people's applause of Putin and his launching of the Ukraine War, which they think provides an example of resisting America's domination and the possibility of reviving an old and once-glorious empire.

Like Jin Xing, famous actress and TV host Ke Lan (柯蓝) has also issued her concern and boycott of the Ukraine War. Ke Lan has an illustrious family background given that her grandfather was one of the founding generals of the PRC, Zhong Qiguang (钟期光). Ke Lan lived in America from the time she was a teenager and was educated there. She did not write any anti-Ukraine War comments herself but relayed others' posts such as those of the famous writer

Beicun (北村), including 'Residents of St Petersburg, you are not soldiers of freedom, you are bloody dictators', and the video clip of a Russian anti-war demonstration that Beicun had posted on his blog. Ke has 2.87 million fans following her blog and owing to her transmission of the anti-Ukraine War comments and videos, her blog has been besieged by netizens who support the Ukraine War, which has resulted in the closure of her blog account (不允许反战的国家：女艺人金星、柯蓝为乌克兰发声被禁言, 2022). Maybe because Jin Xing is married to a German husband and Ke Lan lived and studied in the West, they have developed mindsets that pay more attention to the Western understanding of human rights. Russian and the Chinese people do not have experiences of genuinely democratic rule, and the socialist history of both of the nations advocated and believed in violent revolutions. Moreover, irrational, chaotic and ruthless social and political movements during the heyday of the socialist era have formed a history of brutality, hostility and numbness, which have caused people living in this environment to be unsympathetic and indifferent to other people's suffering and pain.

Different from their grandparents and parents who grew up in the Mao or post-Mao eras, young generations of Chinese lack memories and experiences of the tumultuous and cruel social and political struggles under the rubric of Maoist class struggle and violent revolutions; therefore, they are easily 'educated' by the CCP government as 'Little Pinks' (小粉红), who are young jingoistic Chinese nationalists on the internet. Little Pinks are blind patriots and have no idea of the disastrous past of China under the rule of Mao and his followers. They rarely have any knowledge of the Cultural Revolution, the Anti-rightist Movement, the Great Leap Forward, the Great Famine or the Tiananmen democratic demonstration, because these are all considered by the CCP to be sensitive topics and are banned from media reports and discussions. Unlike those 'Fifty-Cents' (五毛), who are employed commenters or netizens and who earn fifty cents by posting one patriotic comment on social media, Little Pinks truly believe in the party's propaganda and act loyally in protecting the party's image and legitimacy of rule. They often argue with pro-democratic and pro-West netizens on social media platforms regarding controversial and sensitive civil, political and diplomatic issues. Sometimes taking an aggressive or 'wolf warrior' attitude, they sincerely defend the policy and rule of the CCP, and whoever challenges the party's speech or rule will become a target or victim of the Little Pinks' attacks. In contrast to the state's top-down development of an apparatus of paid social media monitors – the 'Fifty-Cent Army' – to shape public opinion (Han 2015 cited in Wong et al. 2021: 2), the Little Pinks are a bottom-up popular nationalist force who blindly defend whatever the Chinese government says and does and fight against any negative news on China. Little Pinks have been enlisted by the Chinese state to form 'a more subtle way in which the state cultivates the tenor of online discourse', and their comments and posts are used as 'user-generated expressions of nationalism' that are amplified whenever possible (Yang 2019: 9 cited in Wong et al. 2021: 4).

Some critics take Little Pinks to be the contemporary version of the Maoist 'Red Guards' (红卫兵), a group of radical revolutionary Chinese youths who recklessly trusted in whatever Mao said and did, which caused much sociopolitical chaos and humanitarian disaster during the peaks of class struggle and political movements. Similar to Mao Zedong (毛泽东), the current Chinese president Xi Jinping (习近平) has long been cultivating his cult of personality among Chinese citizens, particularly the young generations, and resuming Mao's dictatorship while jettisoning the collective leadership that was established during the reign of Deng Xiaoping (邓小平). It has been widely discerned and analysed that in many of China's social, economic and political spheres, Xi is steering a left turn that was initiated by Mao's regime. The emerging closed-door trend is partly because of the outbreak of the Covid epidemic, the vigilant attitude towards the Western world, the call for common prosperity, the ever-tightening control over media reporting and the resumption of Cold War logic in the diplomatic domain. All have indicated that China is going backwards rather than progressing towards political reforms and becoming a democratic country in a real sense. Under these circumstances, 'Little Pinks' and 'Fifty cent-ers' are enlisted and manipulated by the CCP propaganda machine to defend the legitimacy of the party's rule and to lift its soft power on the international stage. Therefore, China needs clear-minded, moral and accountable public intellectuals, opinion leaders and activists to tell people the truth such as the real reasons behind the Ukraine War and the standpoint China should take on this issue. Otherwise, China will be blamed as an accomplice to Putin's invasion and consequently be sanctioned economically by the Western world, which will damage China's international image as a sensible global superpower. Moreover, this will increase hostility from the West, including the European Union and America, and consolidate the Cold War logic in the current world environment that may bring China down economically and politically.

Celebrity writers are another force voicing their concerns and comments as public intellectuals in contemporary China. Celebrity talk show host and writer Gao Xiaosong (高晓松) is representative of these famous men of letters. Gao wears multiple celebrity hats including songwriter, music producer, director, writer, talk show host and bibliophile. Gao emerged from a famous intellectual family background and his grandfather once served as the vice chancellor of Tsinghua University, the number one university in mainland China. Gao himself graduated from Tsinghua, majoring in electronic engineering. However, Gao has a very strong interest in history and is very knowledgeable about Chinese and world histories. In 2012, Gao started to host a talk show programme, *Morning Call* (晓说), which could be viewed on Youku (优酷), one of China's largest online video streaming platforms. The themes and topics of *Morning Call* focus on history, historical and influential figures, cultures and topical issues. Gao's unfathomable knowledge about Chinese and global history, informative and sharp comments on influential historical figures and his eloquent and humorous speaking style have seen him attract and retain a huge fan base.

Through *Morning Call*, Gao offers a rendition of many historical events and issues that is different from the official interpretation and propaganda. He opens the eyes and trains the critical thinking capacity of Chinese audiences, who have long been subjected to the government's explanation of history and historical figures. *Morning Call* can be compared with *Li Ao Has Something to Say* (李敖有话说) in terms of its contents and programme style. Li Ao is a well-known contemporary Taiwanese liberal intellectual and celebrity writer who was jailed for his critical comments on the Taiwanese government ruled by the Nationalist Party. Li was a devoted fighter for media freedom in Taiwan in the 1960s and 1970s, when the Nationalist Party kept tight control of media publications, which made him one of the most famous political activists in Taiwan during that era. Li is a learned scholar of history and he has published around a hundred books, most of which were banned by the Nationalist Party regime under the reign of Chiang Kai-shek (蒋介石) and his son, Chiang Ching-kuo (蒋经国). Li claims that of the past 500 years of Chinese history, he is the author who best uses the vernacular language in writing.

Li's mastery of the Chinese language and his broad collection of archival materials and historical records, plus his good sense of humour, have made his explanations and arguments about historical events and disputes extremely convincing, fascinating and entertaining. Li hosted *Li Ao Has Something to Say* at the influential Hong Kong-based Phoenix satellite TV station from 2004 to 2006. In this successful show he would talk about famous or controversial historical events and stories, which captured the interest of the highbrow audience across the Sinophone world. Through this programme, many mainland viewers were introduced to him, and he became very popular, nicknamed 'Master Li' for his dexterous handling of historical data. Li's mastery of the Chinese language is frequently revealed by his inventive enlistment of erotic and sexual words and phrases to implicate political issues and national events. For example, in *Li Ao Has Something to Say*, he mocked the Nationalist Party's political policy because it 'masturbates Taiwan, and mentally rapes the mainland'. By 'mentally rapes the mainland' he meant that the Nationalist Party lost the mainland to the CCP in 1949, but still harbours the dream of striking back and retaking the mainland; and by 'masturbates Taiwan' he insinuated that the island was under the 'corrupt' rule of the Nationalist Party. In another instance, when Li was jailed by the Nationalist Party regime for his anti-party writings, which endeavoured to create freedom of speech on the island, he adopted a self-mocking manner and said that 'the big head' (here a metaphor for his thought and action) makes mistakes and the 'small head' (here referring to the male sexual organ) suffers, clearly alluding to deprivation of sex when in prison for his open challenge to the dictatorship of the Nationalist Party under the rule of the Chiang family.

Unlike Li Ao, who has taken a clear and utterly anti-government political stance, Gao Xiaosong uses nuanced devices to restore the truth of history and challenge the CCP's narrative. For example, in his programmes, Gao has whitewashed the fame of Chiang Kai-shek and praised his feats in the Anti-Japanese War; restored the fact that the Korean War was precipitated by North Korea's invasion of South Korea; pointed out that America is China's benefactor, the most respected army is the American army and the American army has never come to Chinese land to kill the Chinese people; and suggested that the army directed by the party is called 'Waffen-SS' (implying Hitler's Germany).

Gao's interpretation and comments on history in *Morning Call* were labelled and criticized by the Chinese History Research Institute (中国历史研究院)

as 'historical nihilism' (历史虚无主义). In 2020, in the live-streaming programme *Celebrities Read Classics* (名人读名著), Gao was attacked and smeared by many Chinese netizens via bullet-screen comments, forcing the programme into an emergency shutdown. Those netizens who abused Gao in the programme might constitute 'Little Pinks' and 'Fifty cent-ers' who lack knowledge and insight into history and have long been brainwashed by the official propaganda, or they might harbour extremely strong nationalist sentiment and therefore consider Gao's ideas to be ridiculous and resentful. The gap between China's elite intellectuals and the Chinese people is marked by differences in level of knowledge, intellectual habits and value orientation, laying the foundation for the CCP's obscurantist rule. In 2021, *Morning Call* and others of Gao's books and programmes were taken off the air by Youku, signalling a blocking of Gao Xiaosong by the propaganda machine. Another factor that may have contributed to the banning of Gao Xiaosong was his close relationship with the Chinese private business tycoon, Ma Yun. Ma had recently criticized the Chinese regulatory department that led to his financial technology corporation being pressured by the government. Ma's close friend Zhao Wei in the entertainment world was also implicated and blocked by the government. The cases of Gao Xiaosong and Zhao Wei reflect the natural bonds between the entertainment and business circles and the political turmoil in contemporary China.

At the beginning of the Covid epidemic, between January and March of 2020, well-known writer Fang Fang (方方) published her observations of the outbreak – and everyday people's lives and desperation in the midst of the crisis – on Sina Weibo (新浪微博), the most influential blog channel in mainland China. Fang's writing focused on what she saw and heard during the lockdown of Wuhan (her hometown and the place of origin of the Covid virus) during the epidemic. Her blogs were compiled into a book entitled *Wuhan Diary* (武汉日记) and published in English in America in April 2020. As a result of writing and publishing her Wuhan diary, Fang Fang became the target of attacks from the angry nationalists of China. In her diaries, Fang dared to criticize the government's response to the outbreak of the pandemic. This triggered fierce abuse from nationalists and Little Pinks on Chinese internet platforms. In response to their abuse, Fang said: 'their conduct is just like that of thugs, and they attack whoever does not cooperate with them.' Further, Fang compared the attacks and abuse with the brutal behaviour of

Mao's Red Guards during the Cultural Revolution in the 1960s and 1970s (经济学人：习近平培育了一种丑陋的中国式民族主义, 2022).

Fang's book was then translated into other languages and published in Germany, France, Japan and elsewhere, triggering huge debate and controversy. One of Fang's supporters, famous writer Yan Lianke (阎连科) praised her action thus: 'we should feel grateful to Fang Fang; she raised the status of Chinese writers and literatures'. Professor Tang Yiming (唐翼明) from Central China Normal University commented, 'how come Chinese intellectuals do not take a stand on this kind of event and dare not to speak up? Fang Fang is the most outstanding "war correspondent"!' Another professor, Miao Huaiming (苗怀明), pointed out, 'Fang Fang's diary brings warmth, consolation and so forth to many people and is genuine literature . . . this is the real positive energy (正能量) . . . which will go down in the history of literature and deserves the Nobel Prize for Literature.' American magazine *Diplomat* acclaimed *Wuhan Diary* as the social conscience of Wuhan under lockdown. Another famous Chinese female writer, Zhang Kangkang (张抗抗), supported Fang Fang and compared her with Noam Chomsky, who has insistently critiqued the American government. Negative comments about Fang's *Wuhan Diary* emphasized that Fang's writing was subjective and did not stick to facts; her depictions in the diaries were largely unverified gossip, which was not in line with mainstream Chinese society and did not spread 'positive energy'. Some critics labelled Fang's writing 'Dust Literature' (灰尘文学) and others raised their condemnation to moralistic and political levels: 'Fang's writing reflects a Cold War and Cultural Revolution political standpoint that is hard to accept.' There have also been rumours circulating on the internet that many of Fang's supporters have been reported by netizens for their anti-communist expressions and universities have started to investigate the scholars concerned (看看支持和反对方方的专家都有谁？ 2020). The attention, debate and controversy triggered by Fang's *Wuhan Diary* demonstrate the power of celebrity and their stands as public activists. This can influence public opinion and stimulate independent and critical thinking on the part of Chinese audiences when confronting civil issues and societal crises.

From early 2020 to late 2022, the Chinese government implemented its 'zero COVID' policy, which caused enormous upheaval to the daily life and work of Chinese people. Many lost their jobs as China's economy confronted the biggest attack since the Opening Up period owing to ceaseless lockdowns in major cities such as Beijing and Shanghai.

Reflecting on their suffering and difficulties during the Covid lockdowns, some Chinese people have compared the situation and chaos with that during the Cultural Revolution. They summarize the characteristics of the lockdowns as follows:

1. All levels of local government abuse power; [when] power is out of control there is antagonism between the Party and the masses;
2. Policies conflict with each other, lacking scientific basis; standards have sunk to the bottom;
3. Mobilise the masses to struggle the masses; factions afflict the whole country;
4. Absurd and despicable events emerge one after another, causing widespread harm; cries of discontent rise from all social strata; [people] complaining to high heaven as tragedies break out.
5. The economy declines and people's lives are hard and impoverished;
6. Politics in command, grossly exaggerate things to the level of principle and ideological line; once the key link is grasped, everything will fall into place; common knowledge, general rules, common sense, are all dead;
7. Handle people and matters like a sport; sweep away all voices of doubt and opposition.

> Have the seven points above not appeared of late? The Cultural Revolution is resurrected.

(‘上海 留下一篇篇刻骨铭心的血泪文章’, 2022)

This Cultural Revolution-style lockdown management and control reminded Chinese people of the horrible and irrational movements and struggles of the socialist heyday under the rule of Mao and his followers. As a loyal and stubborn disciple of Mao, current Chinese president Xi Jinping has used the pandemic prevention policies to test the Chinese people's attitude towards his authoritarian rule, which marks a new step taken by him to lead China back to the socialist course that proved a failure during the Mao era. Strict and unscrupulous surveillance of the traditional media and social media outlets makes the struggles of those conscientious public opinion leaders and political activists even harder, whether internet influencers or popular celebrities or stars.

Like Fang Fang, the American-based celebrity writer Yan Geling (严歌苓) has fulfilled her role as a public intellectual and activist when Chinese citizens' safety and rights have been in danger or violated. Yan Geling enjoys stardom in current China, and her works deserve careful study because of their status as 'popular consumer goods' in the present-day Chinese cultural-media marketplace. Although based in America, Yan's novel creations have become the most popular sources of television and film adaptations in mainland China. For example, her novels *Happiness Is Knocking at the Door* (幸福来敲门) and *Tielihua* (铁梨花) have been adapted into television drama serials with the same titles, which enjoy vast popularity in the mainland region; her novel *The Flowers of War* (金陵十三钗) was adapted into a feature film by Zhang Yimou in 2011; also, Yan served as the screenwriter for Chen Kaige's (陈凯歌, another representative figure of Chinese fifth-generation directors) 2008 film, *Forever Enthralled* (梅兰芳). In 2014, Yan Geling's novel *The Criminal Lu Yanshi* (陆犯焉识) was adapted into an art-house blockbuster by Zhang Yimou, *Coming Home* (归来). As one of the most popular celebrity writers of China, which brings her enormous fame and profit, Yan spoke out on the Chained Woman issue during a video talk with professor Zhou Xiaozheng (周孝正). Zhou is a sociologist, historian and former professor of Renmin University of China (人民大学). In recent years, Zhou has emerged as a public intellectual who openly challenges the policies of the CCP. For example, during an interview conducted with a foreign media outlet, he criticized the One Child Policy; he expressed to the *Voice of America* that during the 4th June repression, the Chinese army fired on the people and killed approximately one thousand and that this movement suspended Deng Xiaoping's democratic political reformation; and he commented that the smog pollution in China was a man-made disaster caused by a problematic outlook on development. Because of his outspokenness and candid comments on the social ills of present-day China, Zhou now lives in America. In 2021, Zhou received verbal notification of his dismissal from Renmin University, which Zhou believes is punishment unleashed on him by the CCP government as he dared to articulate his ideas and continued to do so after moving to America. However, Zhou expressed that he did not regret his words and emphasized that freedom of speech is a basic human right that he deserves.

During Yan Geling and Zhou Xiaozheng's virtual conversation about the incident of the rural woman who had been chained and abducted (and then became a hot topic on social media and online discussion channels in early 2022), Yan concurred with Zhou's comment that Xi Jinping was a human trafficker given that he allowed this kind of thing to happen in today's China. Further, Yan smeared Xi by using the word 'fucking' (他妈的), thereby showing her pluck and potentially jeopardizing her career development in mainland China. Yan also published an article commenting on the Chained Woman incident, articulating concerns about the safety and human rights of Chinese women and mocking the government's attitude on this issue and its dereliction of duty (周孝正严歌苓视频对话 '母亲啊母亲': 批评习近平就是个人贩子, 2022).

Apart from the mainland region, there are celebrity activists in Hong Kong who dare to express their civic and political demands and suffer the punishments unleashed on them by the CCP regime. For example, the Hong Kong-based Cantopop singer Denise Ho (何韵诗) has been blacklisted by the Ministry of Culture for her associations with the Umbrella and Sunflower movements or 'pro-independence' opinions (Sullivan and Kehoe 2018: 249). Like rights-defence lawyers and political dissidents, celebrities and stars who act as public and political activists are doomed to be monitored and punished by the Chinese government. Though their endeavours to fight for human, civic and political rights for the Chinese people have not yet achieved their goals, at least we can see an emerging tendency and small sparks here and there that have the potential to inspire the Chinese people to speak up and stand up to defend those rights that they deserve but have long been deprived of.

Sports celebrity as national and political symbol

Researchers acknowledge the complicated and varied roles that contemporary sporting celebrities occupy as 'athletic laborers, entertainers, marketable commodities, role models, and political figures' within an increasingly global cultural economy (Andrews and Jackson 2001: 9). Sports stars themselves gladly utilize their own fame to represent various and conflicting causes, which results in the situation that 'both the production and consumption of these sports-celebrity images vary depending on the particular socio-historical contexts' (Frost 2011: 7). In other words, sports stars are socially constructed, the inventions of both particular historical moments and wider and growing discourses of celebrity have become transnational in reach. For example, in wartime Japan, symbols of sports stars facilitated Japan's 'emergence into the putatively universal realm of sports, unsettled orthodox notions of gender, and facilitated the wartime mobilisation of physically fit men and women' (Frost 2011: 3). Moreover, the demise of a Japanese wrestler evoked a countrywide wave of grief among the Japanese people (Frost 2011).

In Argentina, Archetti (2001) explains how the numerous calamities in Maradona's career came to be understood through a haunting figuration of Argentinian national identity that underscored his status as a national icon. In Canada, Steven Jackson reveals how the popular representation and perception of Canadian ice hockey star Wayne Gretzky signifies the national identity crisis in Canada in the late 1980s. For many Canadians, the signing of the Free Trade Agreement (FTA) with the United States can be regarded as the latest expression of American cultural and economic colonization and will jeopardize the existence and future of Canadian culture, identity and sovereignty. The case of Gretzky exemplifies how extremely visible sporting celebrities are inevitably associated with a dialectic interaction with the national cultural environment in which they operate (Jackson 2001). In addition, scholars have noted how Black sports stars have challenged the Occidental gaze and the conventional Western ways of considering the Black body through their outstanding achievements on the world stage. They have become the first postcolonial athletes, whose actions encompassed international political action against a colonizing power and its legacy (Bale 2001).

In socialist China, industry was nationalized, the monetary economy was curtailed and sport was funded by the state to demonstrate national strength (Jeffreys 2012). Since the early 1950s, sporting celebrities have been made into national heroes and had various connections with Chinese politics. Sports activities and wins provide an effective nexus where state and popular nationalist sentiments merge, mixing patriotic and nationalist discourse with entertainment discourse. A number of the most stirring moments in Chinese sporting history have been imbued with patriotic and nationalist passion. As Dayan and Katz point out, 'Sports, as a media event, are ceremonial politics that "expresses the yearning for togetherness, for fusion"' (Dayan and Katz 1992: viii and 15 cited in Lee 2003: 5). At the 26th session of the World Table Tennis Games held in Beijing in 1961, the Chinese sportsman beat his foreign competitors at a critical moment and lifted the national morale of the Chinese. Athlete Xu Yunsheng's (徐云生) excellent performance galvanized the confidence and determination of the Chinese government and people and displayed it to the whole world, right when Beijing needed to show its strength and power because enmity with the West was as strong as ever before. Sun notes that there is a connection between an individual athlete's attainment and the collective national emotion. The triumph of individual Chinese players is coupled with that of the nation, and there is a shared yearning to read sports events as both similes and metonyms for China's significance in a global context (Sun 2002: 123). In the American case, scholars have pointed out that 'no statistically significant difference was found in the country's reputation effects of the athlete and political leader, suggesting that sports stars have an international influence on par with national political leaders' (Yoo, Lee and Jin 2018: 127).

The explicit connection between sporting glory and national pride shows the political implications of sports. Maoist propaganda merged sporting enthusiasm with revolutionary zeal, for example, and it is precisely this intentional combination which blurs the boundary between political preaching and the competitive spirit of sporting events. In the early 1970s, because of the deteriorating relationship with the Soviet Union, China adjusted its diplomatic relationship with America in a world dominated by Cold War logic. China's ping-pong diplomacy helped to break the ice with America in the political, diplomatic and cultural domains. The use of sports activities in diplomacy has proven successful in the trajectory of politics of socialist China.

Chinese soccer has always been a national trauma given it has never recorded achievements that are enough for the Chinese people to feel proud of. However, Chinese soccer's 'scar' status in the heart of many Chinese people has proved its unifying strength as a sports activity. There is no disparity between Chinese soccer followers and their counterparts elsewhere in the world, as for them the soccer competition is not only a sports contest but also an emblem of state honour. Obviously, chatting about soccer has greater public appeal than discussing politics or ideology, and patriotic and nationalist instruction directed through recreational activities is more efficient than spreading ideology via educational and propaganda devices. Particularly for the younger generation of Chinese people, soccer serves as a good medium in terms of triggering patriotic fervour.

Like Western soccer hooligans, the appalling loss, massive emotional frustration and mutilated national honour drive young Chinese soccer fans to go to unreasonable lengths. It is reported that after a soccer match, a group of young Chinese fans grabbed a foreign's reporter and shouted: 'Tell me which team is better? The Chinese team or the Hong Kongese team? I will kill you if you pick the wrong one.' Soccer has long been granted figurative connotations by people of different countries. For China in particular, soccer has been enlisted to symbolize a castrated man, as the Chinese national soccer team has rarely performed to the expectations of the Chinese people and never won any major international tournament; therefore, Chinese national confidence, reverence and pride have been castrated. Thus, this sort of vindictive and illogical action by young Chinese soccer fanatics bears a resemblance to the Wang Qiming type of Chinese masculinity in *Beijingers in New York* (北京人在纽约), a popular TV drama show released in mainland China at the beginning of the 1990s. The 'screw your foreigners' impulse examined by Geremie Barmé (1995) represents the recovered and rebuilt national pride and spirit of the Chinese people. As Wu has pointed out, 'Nationalism is a super ideology. It encompasses and transcends other forms of philosophical paradigms, political ideologies and religious beliefs. Once it comes into being, it exists as its own cause and only follows its own rationale' (Wu 2007: 117). This exactly illuminates the absurd and hysterical reaction of young Chinese soccer fans when a nationalist feeling is sparked.

In 1986, the competition for the primary rafting right of China's longest river, the Yangtze (长江), took place between Chinese sportsmen and their foreign counterparts. A sense of a collective victimhood and national crisis emerged out of the competition. Guo has sharply commented: 'the image of China-as-victim serves a domestic political purpose [and] . . . the inculcation of a sense of victimhood is designed to enhance an awareness that past humiliations can be repeated if China remains technologically backward and becomes politically divided' (Guo 2004: 34). It is easy to identify here an apparent political logic that endorses the CCP's authority and legitimacy in keeping the Chinese nation united and Chinese society stable and prosperous. In this way, an ordinary sports activity can be highly politicized and ideologized in the Chinese sociopolitical context.

When Hong Kong returned to Chinese sovereignty, another sports activity was enlisted and hijacked that illustrates sports celebrity's symbolic function in the political sphere. In 1997, Hong Kongese celebrity Ke Shouliang's (柯受良) adventure driving over the Tiger Leaping Gorge of the Yellow River (黄河虎跳峡) was regarded as symbolizing the return of sovereignty of Hong Kong to the PRC. This activity allegorically and powerfully depicted the thrill of coming back to the mother's embrace and returning to one's motherland, which concluded with the celebrity's symbolic jump that signified reunification and the resurgence of the nation. The patriotism/ethnic Chineseness and the entertainment appeal of the Hong Kong-based star's jump demonstrate the usual ways in which Hong Kong celebrities are employed to gain political trust in the CCP regime. This function serves as a prerequisite for their popularity in the mainland region. Hong Kong stars seem to either politically support the mainland government (such as Jackie Chan 成龙), or remain silent on political issues (such as Andy Lau 刘德华). However, Chan's course may have repercussions, as 'he has lately found himself alienating fans with his overtly political statements, such as the controversial "The Chinese need to be controlled" ("zhongguoren xuyao guanli") statement' (Jacobs 2009; Weiss 2013: 230).

The end of the colonial history of Hong Kong has been employed as a pivotal icon to mark the end of China's history of humiliation. The unification of the

Chinese nation is a vital tactic utilized by the CCP to form its united front, which is of importance in strengthening its legitimacy. In the most recent years, the CCP's ambition to militarily retake Taiwan could be considered a further development of this approach, which will not only consolidate the CCP's rule of the whole Chinese territory but also lessen the resentment of the Chinese people as victims of humiliation.

China's success in the 2001 bid to host the 2008 Olympic Games pushed the nationalist sentiment and emotion of the Chinese citizens to its zenith. As Dayan and Katz have observed, 'Within China, the mass-mediated Olympic Games will enhance the status of the authorities and integrate social groups, as all eyes are "fixed on the ceremonial center"' (Dayan and Katz 1992: viii, 15 cited in Lee 2003: 5). Sun further commented that the Olympic Games had the potential to manufacture numerous moments of success and delight, which could be effortlessly turned into political spectacles to amass political capital for the CCP to use for several tactical desires, including sponsoring nationalism and growing its political validity (Sun 2002: 126). Wins in the sports domain have been employed as symbols of strength and power by the Chinese government to promote its idea of resurrecting the Chinese nation in hope that it will overcome internal malaises and salvage its declining authority. It was the state's intention that winning the right to stage the 2008 Olympic Games would make all other problems fade into the background and that all other social problems and national missions, including building democracy, combating social injustice and promoting individual rights, would be superseded by a rising nationalism. As a Sohu Web (搜狐网) documentary *In Search of Modern China* (追寻现代中国) commented:

> We must unite together, and put all our efforts into building a more powerful and confident nation. We should stop entangling ourselves with the trivial concerns of life and the gain and loss of individuals. We should make sacrifices and contribute to maintain the long-term stability and continued prosperity of our nation. When the year 2008 comes, we will be able to show the world the most excellent achievements and the greatest power of our nation.

Here, the individual was made to seem inconsequential and irrelevant, and it was argued that they should be willing to forego themselves for the nation. On a platform provided by China's commercial online media such as Sohu

Web, the customary discourse of Chinese state nationalism illuminated by classic slogans ultimately became apparent at a critical moment in China's sports history. It is difficult to find a more appropriate moment to convey and underscore patriotic and nationalist sentiment than when the Chinese Olympic dream came true. Thus, sports activities, celebrities and stars have a natural and innate connection with state propaganda and Chinese politics. In the history of socialist China, if Chinese athletes changed their nationality and competed on behalf of other nations, they have been mocked and despised by Chinese citizens as traitors, or at least people who do not love their country. Particularly when these sportsmen have competed against Chinese athletes in the international arena, they have stimulated enormous hatred from Chinese audiences, who take sport as not only a game but also a political issue. In other words, defectors in the sporting world are seen as politically problematic and disloyal to their motherland, which offers another example of the 'hijacked' status of sports events and celebrities in the political atmosphere of socialist China.

In recent times, media and public attention has been given to those athletes with both Chinese and foreign backgrounds or nationalities who have chosen to represent China in international games, and this has won applause and favour from Chinese citizens. For example, the grandson and granddaughter of a famous high jump athlete during the Mao era, Zheng Fengrong (郑凤荣), have given up their Canadian nationality and represented China in international sports competitions. Zheng Fengrong was a legendary figure in the sports history of socialist China because she was the first Chinese athlete to break a world record after the founding of the PRC. Zheng met with the then CCP chairman Mao Zedong (毛泽东) and the Chinese premier Zhou Enlai (周恩来). She named her grandson Zheng Enlai (郑恩来) to show her admiration for Premier Zhou.

China's National Department of Sport (国家体育总局) and the Chinese Olympic Committee （中国奥委会） called for overseas Chinese athletes to participate in the 2020 Summer Olympic Games and the 2022 Winter Olympic Games. In response to this call, Zheng Enlai and his younger sister, Zheng Ni'nali (郑妮娜力), both decided to give up their Canadian nationality and make their contribution to the Chinese sports cause. Zheng Ni'nali speaks fluent Chinese, and she has expressed that her dream is to win a medal for China in the Olympic Games. During the 2021 Tokyo Olympic Games, Zheng

Ni'nali had the top score for Chinese sportspeople in women's heptathlon. In the 2022 Beijing Winter Olympic Games, Zheng Enlai proudly represented China in the national ice hockey team. The illustrious family background and their patriotic spirit have won the Zheng brother and sister popularity and admiration in China, and they have reinforced the bond between sports and nationalistic sentiment within current China's political atmosphere. Another popular overseas-turned-Chinese athlete is Eileen Gu (谷爱凌). In the 2022 Winter Olympic Games held in Beijing, the young Gu, who possesses both American and Chinese nationality, represented China. She won many medals in the Winter Olympic Games, putting her in the spotlight of Chinese media, which proclaimed her to be a Chinese national hero full of patriotic sentiment.

Zheng Enlai and Eileen Gu's participation in the 2022 Beijing Winter Olympic Games and the loyalty and patriotic passion they have demonstrated in front of the Chinese people have not only put them directly in the spotlight of the Chinese media but also diverted the Chinese public's attention away from the diplomatic boycott of the Beijing Winter Olympic Games by major Western countries. Several weeks prior to the opening of the Beijing Winter Olympic Games, the United States, Britain and Australia called for a diplomatic boycott of the games in light of China's poor human rights record, including the CCP's inhumane treatment of the Xinjiang Uyghur minority and rights-defence lawyers. Together with China's poor performance in handling the Covid epidemic at the beginning of the outbreak and its uncooperative attitude in the search for the origins of the virus, China's international image has deteriorated sharply in recent times and its relationship with the Western world has almost hit rock bottom. Back in 2008 when Beijing was holding its first Olympic Games, the international society had great expectations that the games would lead the Chinese government to become more responsible and humane. However, before the games opened, there erupted violent protests against the repressive policies implemented by the CCP government in Tibet; consequently, around thirty Tibetans were jailed and some were sentenced to life imprisonment.

Undoubtedly, through the 2008 Olympic Games, particularly its extravagant opening ceremony, Beijing showed the world its economic achievement and the historical honour of the Chinese nation; moreover, it demonstrated China's soft power and verified that China had become a superpower on the international stage. Some historians and cultural critics even considered the success of the

2008 Olympic Games to signify the 'revival of the Chinese nation'. However, the 2008 Olympic Games also exposed the naivety of the international community in believing that sports would bring about political reformation. The 2008 Olympic Games succeeded despite the ever-deteriorating human rights records of China and its ever-increasing autocratic rule, as evident in the enforced Hong Kong National Security Law (香港国安法) and the tightening control and suppression of political dissidents. This should cause sports fans, athletes, corporate sponsors and the broader global community to question the International Olympic Committee's decision to grant the rights to host the games to a despotic state. Consequently, if the International Olympic Committee wants to maintain its image of protecting human rights, it should reconsider its criteria for awarding the rights to host the Olympic Games. Judging from historical experience, diplomatic boycotts from the West will not prompt the Chinese government to repair its damaged international image; on the contrary, they could make the CCP government more aggressive (分析: 北京冬奥会召开在即　中国能否挽回不良国际影响). Taking the current Ukraine War as an example, the CCP government – especially under the rule of Xi Jinping, who has been widely recognized as a single-minded and wilful person – is reluctant to change its attitude towards the Ukraine War and acknowledge its nature as an unjust invasion. In addition, the Chinese government has endeavoured to support Russia's Ukraine War propaganda and block its citizens' access to Western media coverage of the war.

Like the Russian people, who will be sentenced to up to fifteen years in prison if they protest against the Ukraine War, Chinese people will receive legal punishment if they 'act wantonly' and 'issue groundless criticism' of the central government's decisions and policies (妄议中央决定与政策). The Chinese are one of the most obedient peoples in the world because they have been admonished to behave and impose self-discipline under the totalitarian rule of the CCP since the founding of the PRC. In particular, athletes have long been receiving physical training and moral education and discipline to respect the rules of collectivism and maintain loyalty to their country.

Here, the cohort of Chinese athletes might usefully illustrate how power cascades through individuals in Chinese society. In *Discipline and Punish*, Foucault explored how power operates at a microphysical level through the disciplined training of human bodies. Consistent with his comments on power as relationships and networks, Foucault (1979: 25–7) pointed out that the operation of power should be considered a strategy exercised on the body whose effects of domination are attributed to dispositions, manoeuvres, tactics, techniques and functioning through 'the microphysics of power' and 'political technology of the body'. The Foucauldian 'political technology of the body' embodied in 'political physics' and 'political anatomy' is conducted through disciplining the body. This 'discipline of the body' is 'a policy of coercions that act upon the body, a calculated manipulation of its elements, its gestures, its behavior. The human body was entering a machinery of power that explores it, breaks it down and rearranges it' (Foucault 2005: 136–8).

According to Foucault (1980), power should be considered a synaptic system, which enters the skin of human bodies and is engraved in their behaviour, attitude and speech. Consequently, this 'mechanics of power' manufactures docile bodies through regular disciplining, inspection and training. The implementation of power within human bodies occurs through systems and institutions such as factories, armies and schools, with the help of a series of skills, technologies and procedures; thus, individuals are successfully regulated, disciplined and manipulated. According to Foucault's theory, Chinese athletes impose self-discipline on their body, speech, attitudes and thoughts while receiving training in the national sports teams and competing in the international sports arena; during this process, they are brainwashed, controlled and manipulated. Because of their sports stardom and their specific political connection with the honour of the Chinese state, they exemplify for the Chinese people how power works on individual Chinese citizens and their relationship with their government and country. Chinese athletes are among the most trustworthy devotees of the CCP and the Chinese nation. They have been modelled as the embodiment of the fame and glory of their country and shoulder great political obligation; their personal success and defeat are worth nothing when compared with that of the collective and the nation.

In major international sporting competitions, Chinese athletes are often ordered by their coach to be purposely defeated by their own teammate in order to ensure that the Chinese national team obtains the best overall athletic results. For a long time, no Chinese athletes dared to expose this embarrassing and unfair situation. Some took it as normal and reasonable because they had been educated for so many years that they should prioritize the collective and the nation's honour over their own; these athletes rarely considered this 'totalitarian rule' in the Chinese local and national sports teams as an offence to their individual rights, as they might be dismissed from national sports teams or face punishment if they did so. However, in the most recent years, indications of a changed political ecology in the sporting world have become clear with the emergence of sports stars who expose the corrupt culture in sports. These individuals bring into question the morality and legitimacy of the Chinese government as they consider the scandals and chaos in the micro sports circle to mirror the corruption and pandemonium in the macro social and political domains. Such voicing of concern from sports celebrities illustrates new ways that sporting stars could contribute to the building of an equal and sound society under the rule of law.

It is argued nowadays that China was under totalitarian rule during the Maoist era. However, this fact was not clear back to 1951 when Arendt published *The Origins of Totalitarianism*. In her preface to the third part of the book, Arendt was unsure whether the Chinese case (Maoist China) justified inclusion in her study of totalitarianism. However, the absence of the Chinese context in her book was due primarily to the shortage and uncertainty of knowledge about China in the Western world at the time of Arendt's research; China had isolated itself from the outside world after its successful revolution (Arendt 1986: xxvi). Arendt mentions in her book that in Maoist China, 'thought rectification' is carefully controlled and is a constant 'molding and remolding of the minds' of almost the whole Chinese population. However, at the time of writing *The Origins of Totalitarianism*, Arendt lacked knowledge about this process: how it was practised in everyday life, who would conduct the 'remolding' and what the consequences were of the 'brainwashing' in terms of whether it caused any conversions of people's character (Arendt 1986: xxvi).

In China at that time, intellectuals, especially those liberal-minded ones, were the main targets of the 'thought rectification' movement, and the re-education farms were where the regime implemented 'thought rectification'. Besides constant preaching and propaganda, heavy labour and starvation were employed as useful and crucial methods by which to implement the 'thought rectification', which obviously was more impactful in transforming the personality and 'beliefs' of the intellectuals. In other words, the transformation of the intellectuals' thought was actually conducted through their body. Under pressure to eke out a bare existence, the Chinese intellectuals deserted their valued principles. According to Dikötter (2010: xiv), during the peak of the Great Famine between 1958 and 1962, 'the very survival of an ordinary person came increasingly to depend on the ability to lie, charm, hide, steal, cheat, pilfer, forage, smuggle, trick, manipulate or otherwise outwit the state'. Here, Dikötter's observation about the general population of China during the Great Famine also applies to the intellectuals in the re-education farms. Mao not only destroyed the physical conditions of the Chinese intellectuals but also dispossessed them of their right to live as people of integrity and worth.

It is widely observed that in the recent decade under the rule of Xi Jinping, tighter political and media controls and surveillance have been implemented in both mainland China and Hong Kong. This has pushed contemporary Chinese intellectuals into a more embarrassing circumstance, which has made them become either silenced or defamed if they issue criticism against the Chinese government and its leaders. The totalitarian rule of the CCP has of course claimed to invite dissenting opinions, however not many influential figures – including public intellectuals – have dared to voice them, unless they are based overseas; otherwise they will be punished, banned and 'disappeared' from public view.

However, on 4 June 2020, which was the 31st anniversary of the 1989 Tiananmen democratic protests, two famous and successful Chinese athletes Hao Haidong (郝海东) and his wife Ye Zhaoying (叶钊颖) openly criticized the corruption of the Chinese government and condemned its one-party rule in a video interview that was published on YouTube. Hao was a former football player in the Chinese national soccer team and one of the most well-known strikers in Asia. Ye was a former badminton world champion. Both are outspoken and famous for their upright personality. In their video interview, the couple's comments ranged from the mismanagement and corruption in the Chinese professional sporting world to the chaos in Hong Kong, which deeply worried and upset them and led them to propose the idea of founding a 'New Federal State of China' (新中国联邦). Their opinion was that the chaos and aberrant situations in the Chinese sporting world were a sign of the broader corruption in Chinese society. It was the bureaucrats and government that impaired the political, commercial and social ecology of the whole nation by ignoring the rules and laws. Under the rubric of the 'New Federal State of China', they proposed the rule of law and democratic rights of the Chinese citizens.

According to Arendt, one significant feature of totalitarianism is its complete contempt for law. The guidelines and sanctions of a legal code are no impediment to totalitarian rule, as what is legal or lawful is really only the will of the party and its leadership (Arendt 1986). In the recent history of communist China, the *laojiao* system (劳教制度) has sent the strongest signal of the dictatorial regime's disregard of law. The *laojiao* system literally refers to receiving education through labour. It imprisons and exploits people who are not really criminals in any usual understanding of the word. In contemporary China, many of the *laojiao fenzi* (劳教分子; people who receive education through labour) are political dissidents or those who have a different opinion on the political system to the party – they have not broken any laws of China. Therefore, the *laojiao* system itself is a 'law' fashioned by the Maoist regime, which actually goes against the spirit of laws. The unique existence of the *laojiao* system can be traced back to Maoist China and up to current China, making it clear that totalitarian rule is still ongoing. The Xinjiang Re-education Camps (新疆再教育营), which are named by the Chinese government as Vocational Education and Training Centers (职业技能教育培训中心), or Counter-extremism Centres (去极端化培训中心), are actually labelled by media outside of China as concentration camps (集中营) or internment camps (拘留所). These internment camps were rebuilt from schools or other government facilities and aim to re-educate those Uyghurs who have been impacted by extremist thoughts but have not committed any actual misconduct or crimes. In the internment camps, the students study the common language of the nation, legal knowledge and professional skills to help them return to 'normal' life. It is reported by overseas media that the Chinese government has seized hundreds of thousands of Uyghurs in the internment camps that are spread all over Xinjiang Province.

Many scholarly works about celebrities and politics explore whether the rise of celebrity politics trivializes the public sphere. Some others note that celebrities manage to shift the tone of communications towards a more personalized and dramatied style (Meyer 1995 cited in Thrall et al. 2008: 364). Scholars have also pointed out that sports and politics should be defined. A stream of research on athletes' activism has shown people's reactions to athletes' protests, which have suggested that people find sports and politics to be irreconcilable, and fans do not assess athletes' activism favourably, considering that activism is not a part of an athlete's duties (Frederick, Sanderson and Schlereth 2017; Gill 2016; Sanderson, Frederick and Stocz 2016; Kaufman 2008; Jain, Sharma and Behl 2021). Moreover, in reality, celebrities very delicately choose which issues to advocate, bringing prominence to only the most politically uncontroversial issues (though there are some exceptions) (Meyer 1995). Also, 'celebrities tend to align with liberal perspectives on issue debates, focus on charity or fundraising efforts rather than on real political reform' (Becker 2013: 2). Here, Hao and Ye's advocacy of the founding of a 'New Federal State of China' could be considered an 'exception' to the pattern of celebrity activists' choices. They openly announced their political tenets and ideas, which rarely happens in China's sports and entertainment circles. Though Hao and Ye's action might risk their favour and popularity among their fans, they achieved a more meaningful goal, namely to rally the Chinese people to resist totalitarian rule and to defend their human and political rights.

Hao and Ye's proposal of a 'New Federal State of China' was endorsed by the Chinese political activist and dissident Miles Kwok (郭文贵) and a former political strategist in the Trump administration, Steve Bannon. Kwok is an exiled Chinese entrepreneur who was one of the richest businessmen in China. He was accused by the Chinese government of bribery, kidnapping, money laundering and other misdeeds, and to dodge these allegations, he fled to America in 2014. Kwok made his fortune out of the construction projects associated with the 2008 Beijing Olympic Games. Kwok's business scandals were revealed because one of his political connections lost power and faced seizure of his assets. During his time in America, Kwok allied with Bannon in initiating the 'revelation' movement (爆料运动), which publicized some unverified 'confidential documents of the Chinese government'. These documents revealed China's connection and cooperation with North Korea in solving nuclear issues, which attracted enormous attention from the government, media and people of China and the world.

Kwok started his 'revelation' movement by charging Chinese officials with immorality via his YouTube live monologues and Twitter channel, with the intention of destabilizing the Chinese authorities. On the eve of the 31st anniversary of the 4th June Tiananmen democratic protest, Kwok and Bannon joined the event announcing the founding of the 'New Federal State of China' that aimed to overthrow the Chinese government, which also featured Hao Haidong and his wife Ye Zhaoying. Kwok's whistle-blower image and his 'revelation' campaign stimulated chaos in mainland China and America and was reported by American mainstream media outlets including *The New York Times*, *Financial Times* and *Forbes*. In 2018, the Chinese state accused Kwok of forging government documents by enticing others to fake confidential official documents issued by national-level state organizations. These forged documents concerned not only national issues including military defence, diplomatic matters and fiscal directives but also the personal information of central and provincial government officials such as their illegitimate children, concubines and luxury housing.

Kwok's motivation for defaming the Chinese government and officials was perhaps understandable because he might have been implicated in factional struggles within political circles owing to his close bonds with some high-level government officials. However, Hao and Ye's anti-Chinese government behaviour and speech confounded the Chinese authorities. They were the most politically disciplined cohort of citizens in contemporary China, athletes – famed ones who had won national and international championships. That they stepped forward to boldly condemn the Chinese government violated the traditional functions of sports figures and stars as enlisted by the CCP to mobilize Chinese people and spread its propaganda. In this sense, Hao and Ye's rebellious action marked a watershed in the relationship between Chinese athletes and their government and nation. Truly, for many Chinese people, their behaviour is no longer considered a betrayal of their country but rather a valiant attitude and manner that vents steam for many Chinese people.

Hao and Ye expressed in an interview with *The Wall Street Journal* that there were many Chinese people who harboured the same thoughts as they did but lacked the guts to articulate them within Chinese borders given their voice had been neglected and suppressed by the government for ages. In the same interview, the athlete couple recapped their concern and critique of the totalitarian rule of the Chinese government and their readiness to promote human rights even at the cost of probable political and personal sacrifice (Wong 2020). Needless to say, Hao and Ye's defiant behaviour and speech invited criticism and punishment from the CCP: all references to them on Chinese websites were removed and the Weibo accounts of Hao and Ye were deleted, together with their professional profiles on major Chinese internet portals. Though their voice and political opinions may have been overshadowed by various discussions about their motivations for speaking up for Chinese athletes and Chinese people, the fact that their voice had been heard at all marked a watershed moment in the history of Chinese sports.

One year later, in November 2021, Chinese female tennis player Peng Shuai (彭帅) accused a retired member of the Standing Committee of the CCP Politbureau, Zhang Gaoli (张高丽), of sexual harassment. Peng published an entry on Sina Blog (新浪微博) exposing the abnormal sexual relationship between herself and Zhang, who was one of the highest-level Chinese leaders in the history of socialist China. Peng's accusation of Zhang was considered another ground-breaking event in the history of contemporary China and escalated from a personal dispute between Peng and Zhang to a political level, which arguably marked a politicizing tendency in sports. Peng's charge of Zhang attracted attention from international sports figures and society and governments of many countries, which led to the cancellations of matches in mainland China and Hong Kong by the Women's Tennis Association (WTA) and the diplomatic boycott of the Beijing Winter Olympic Games by many Western governments, headed by the United States. Peng's revelation also sheds light on the problematic ecology involving the exchange of power and sex between the Chinese career field and officialdom. In present-day China, many CCP government officials have involved themselves in trading in power and sex. The women normally receive a promotion following their affair with the leaders in their organizations or with other powerful, high-ranking government officials.

A publicized case in 2014 involved Zhou Yongkang, the former minister of the Ministry of Public Security and secretary of Political and Legislative Affairs Committee of the CCP Central Committee, who was also a former member of the Politburo Standing Committee of the CCP Central Committee (retired in 2012). Zhou reportedly had affairs with two China Central Television (CCTV) hosts. One of these presenters was promoted to the position of deputy director of the Information Centre of the Political and Legislative Affairs Committee of the CCP Central Committee. It has been reported that among the major cases involving government officials at a ministerial level, almost every case investigated by procurators entailed some form of trading in power and sex (Jeffreys 2006).

On one hand, these scandals reveal the extreme moral decadence of high-ranking CCP officials. In addition, they reflect the desperate pursuit of power, reputation and materialistic enjoyment by these famous women of China. Besides the sex-related corruption involving high-ranking CCP officials, virtually every corrupt official in China has a mistress or second wife, according to investigations conducted by the CCP's Central Commission for Discipline Inspection and the All-China Women's Federation (Xie 2003 cited in Jeffreys 2006). In light of this situation, some legal experts in China proposed the criminalization of the sex-related bribery and corruption engulfing the Chinese political world. Zhao Dengju, who was China's deputy procurator-general, affirmed that criminalizing the practice of sexual bribery and corruption would become an imperative device in China's continued battle against corruption. This would contribute further to existing legal and judicial reform in the name of strengthening China's current move to a 'rule of law'. Although this proposition supporting the proscription of sex-related bribery and corruption persistently receives extensive media attention in China, it was eventually rejected by the National People's Congress (Jeffreys 2006: 159–62).

In recent years, the mistress or 'third party' has emerged as a new force in the anti-corruption battle. This new way of revealing the corrupted morality of CCP cadres follows the path of a mass-line political campaign, initiated during early stages of socialist China with a promise of a 'cleaner government' and the abolition of corruption. The mass-line campaigns mobilized the public to report on and disparage cadre misconduct rather than relying on organizations like the courts and the police. Through the adoption of this mass-line movement to eliminate corruption, the Maoist government did succeed in exerting a high level of regulation over the actions of government officers (Li 2001: 573–86 cited in Jeffreys 2006: 170).

The current campaign to overthrow corrupt cadres, as initiated by their mistresses, follows both a top-down propaganda mechanism and a bottom-up populist trend. On one hand, the Chinese Central Government adopts a banner of 'Combat Corruption on Weibo' and manipulates this social media to spread designated material to stimulate public antipathy towards corrupt officials' abuse of power. On the other hand, the government uses collective pleas on Weibo to castigate the misbehaving officials and impose social justice (Gu 2014: 82).[1] In a situation where there is a lack of legal methods to control the moral deterioration and collapse of corrupt officials, sexuality has taken centre stage as the party utilizes whistle-blowing mistresses and sex scandals as political tools to launch its anti-corruption battle. In other words, the CCP government has enlisted sexual permissiveness as 'a ready and useful hook for nailing officials', 'many of whom have already been prosecuted on the score' (Vaswati 2012).

The mass-line anti-corruption campaign has triggered a controversial debate regarding the protection of corrupt CCP officials' privacy, despite their mistakes and crimes. The legal advocates of the criminalization of sex-related bribery and corruption consider the right of the Chinese general public to a trustworthy and operative government more important than the protection of the privacy of corrupt cadres (Wu 2000 cited in Jeffreys 2006). Another major concern stimulated by the new media-based populist movement of cracking down on corruption revolves around the role of mistresses and 'third parties' of corrupt officials. The official CCP mouthpiece, the *People's Daily*, states that China should not count on angry lovers to fight corruption as 'even though at times, for many reasons, mistresses are led by fallings out with corrupt officials to denounce them, at the root of the issue, both their motives are the same – to satisfy each other's greed' and to 'pin anti-corruption hopes' on the mistresses is 'to go in for evil attacking evil'. The *People's Daily* also states, 'it is not the right path for the will of the people' (Derelict Chinese TV Host Ji Yingnan Reveals 'Treacherous Official' Fan Yue's Lavish Lifestyle, 2013).

Apart from these hidden and potential traps generated by the anti-corruption battle led by mistresses and 'third parties', the campaign relying on 'betrayed' lovers to combat corruption itself is regarded as a crooked method. From a long-term viewpoint, the lack of effective and independent judicial systems and institutions, which is a direct result of one-party rule and dictatorship, constitutes the most momentous reason for the rampancy of corruption within the political and economic domains of China. In the case of Peng and Zhang, Peng revealed in her blog post that Zhang pursued her until she finally fell in love with him. Their relationship was on and off and lasted for more than ten years before Zhang 'played missing' (玩失踪) repeatedly, which made Peng feel that she has been deserted by him. Peng believes that Zhang seduced her only to eventually abandon her. She expressed her anguish in her blog entry thus: 'I feel like I am a walking corpse and running flesh. I am pretending every day and I am not sure which me is the real me? I should not stay alive, however I do not have the guts to die. I want to live a simple life but things do not turn out the way I want.' Assuming that she had been jettisoned by Zhang, Peng was very angry and sad so she published her blog. She knew that her behaviour and attempt was playing with fire but she was still determined to reveal the truth to the public. Peng's post stayed on Sina Blog for twenty minutes before it was deleted; at the same time, Peng's Sina Blog account was banned and relevant reports and searches became sensitive on Chinese websites.

Peng's revelation raised concerns for her safety from the international community as she disappeared from public vision after the publication of her blog post on 2 November. Two weeks later, the international sports society launched the 'Where is Peng Shuai?' campaign on the internet. The chairman of the WTA, Steve Simon, expressed in his announcement that Peng Shuai and all women's voices should be heard, and Peng's case should receive comprehensive, fair and apparent investigation. This attracted attention from the International Tennis Federation and the United Nations. Consequently, reporter Shen Wei posted a recent photo of Peng Shuai on Twitter and the retired chief editor of the *Global Times* (环球时报), Hu Xijin (胡锡进), reposted the photo and published another of Peng Shuai and her friends gathering together at a trending restaurant in Beijing. Later, Hu uploaded a video recording of Peng Shuai attending the opening ceremony of the finals of the Beijing Youth Tennis Games as evidence of her safety and to mitigate the damage from the Peng Shuai accident in the international arena, which had catalysed many political outcomes including the West's diplomatic boycott of the Beijing Winter Olympic Games. However, these photos and videos did not assuage the concerns of the international sporting community about the safety of Peng Shuai. At their request, the Chinese government arranged a video chat between Peng Shuai and the president of the International Olympic Committee, and later the two sides met in Beijing during the Winter Olympic Games.

Perhaps bowing to pressure, Peng wrote an email to the president of WTA expressing that she did not want to be disturbed, and on 19 December, Peng denied in an interview with Singapore's *Lianhe Zaobao* (联合早报) that she had ever said that she was sexually harassed by anyone, and she had been staying in her Beijing home with complete freedom. From the history of the Chinese government's ways of dealing with similar scandals, people have reason to believe Peng's 'clarifications' about her relationship with Zhang Gaoli and her safety were made under the pressure and intimidation of Chinese government officials and public security officers. Her revelations severely damaged the international image of the Chinese government and its high-level officials, which, according to the Chinese government, provided another opportunity for 'foreign hostile forces' to 'attack' China. In the case of Peng, she should not be regarded as a political activist in any real sense; however, her revelation sent shock waves throughout China's sporting and political circles, which consequently damaged the image of the CCP and its legitimacy.

Female rights activism in the world of entertainment

In recent decades, Chinese celebrities and stars and their private lives, family disputes and personal scandals have been serving as lenses through which gender roles and relationships in contemporary China – and Chinese women's rights-defending activities and movements – have been revealed. In the post-socialist and post-revolutionary era, by manufacturing and foregrounding those hardworking, gentle and virtuous female personae represented by celebrity figures in their roles in films and TV dramas, the state propaganda machine seeks to promote the 'good wife and wise mother' (贤妻良母) image of Chinese females. The 1989 classic Chinese television drama *Yearning* (渴望) created the Liu Huifang (刘慧芳) character, who represents almost all the Chinese female merits such as diligence, persistence, sacrifice and responsibility. The actress Zhang Kaili (张凯丽), who played Liu Huifang, has become the embodiment of her role in the drama that garnered enormous appeal among Chinese audiences.

Similarly, in the 1998 TV drama show *Whatever Zhang Damin's Happy Life* (贫嘴张大民的幸福生活), the image of another classic model Chinese woman was produced. The female lead in the show, Li Yunfang (李云芳), was a pretty and kind young woman who married poor worker Zhang Damin. Yunfang's tender, soft and considerate personality, together with her husband's humorous and optimistic temperament, created constant happiness and enjoyment out of the family's impoverished living conditions. In the history of socialist and post-socialist China, celebrities represented and spread 'positive energy' and were enlisted by the propaganda machines to mobilize the public and transmit the government's directives and ideology. While celebrities were used to bolster the governing ideology of their age and were considered instrumental for the conservation of the hegemonic order, they had no control over their own images or the messages they carried to the public (Dyer 2004; Ribke 2015: 2).

During the Cultural Revolution, celebrities lacked control of their own public image and fate, no matter whether they were appointed to star as heroic or revolutionary figures or were unfortunately picked to play capitalist or petit-bourgeois roles in films. Many performers became household names and enjoyed lifelong admiration and popularity because of their positive or red classic roles in revolutionary films; others were critiqued and persecuted when their stage or film roles were classified as 'poisonous weeds' (毒草). The latter were also used by the party as negative examples to educate the revolutionary masses. Chinese women's encounters and experiences in particular historical periods confirm Simone de Beauvoir's words that 'one is not born a woman, one becomes one', which 'highlights the role of culture, norms and expectations in determining the role that women played in society' (Savigny and Warner 2015: 14).

Compared with the socialist, modern-day Chinese celebrities and stars not only have more freedom to choose their roles in films and TV dramas and thereby create their favoured public persona; they also enjoy greater liberty to voice their viewpoints and ideas on topics such as gender, family, social and even political issues via social media platforms. Nowadays, more and more Chinese female celebrities act as advocates for gender equality and Chinese women's rights-defending activities and movements.

For example, many mainland Chinese actresses and celebrity figures such as Xu Jinglei (徐静蕾) and Yu Feihong (俞飞鸿) promote non-married life; others including Mu Zimei (木子美) and Hong Huang (洪晃) eulogize sexual liberation; and even younger-generation female stars have started to advocate feminism, which was a label constantly avoided by Chinese female celebrities and stars. In early 2017, Xu Jiao (徐娇), a younger-generation Chinese female actress, openly called for the public to boycott a not-yet-released film, *Duckweek* (*Chengfengpolang* 乘风破浪, 2017, dir. Han Han), because the theme song of the movie was clearly sexist. Han is widely accepted as a public opinion leader based on his influential blog entries, which contain burning satire of the social ills of contemporary China. However, as scholars have pointed out, Han's films demonstrate a 'celebration of masculinity' and Han's masculinity 'is constructed at the expense of women and non-hegemonic men' (Hunt

2020: 29). In his films 'the recurring image of freewheeling outlaws relies on conservative gender ideals, with the result that women's voices are frequently silenced' (Hunt 2020: 30).

Since Xu Jiao opened up her Weibo account in 2011, she has commented on various social and cultural issues, such as the disappearing seals, and on regulations that forbid using electroshock therapy to 'cure' internet addiction. Xu Jiao has also reported unceasingly on gender-related social and cultural issues. One debate occurred when some of her followers said that they saw her as a tomboy and she openly acknowledged, appreciated and showed her respect for a gender-neutral lifestyle. Xu Jiao openly articulated her agony upon hearing *Duckweed*'s two theme songs, particularly the first song titled *Man's Manifesto* (男子汉宣言), which includes some lyrics that showcase obvious patriarchal sentiment and male chauvinism. Xu considered that as a public figure and as a Chinese female and citizen, she could not keep silent on issues that should have triggered public discussion. Consequently, the celebrity status of Xu significantly stimulated the debate on this feminist subject. Chinese celebrities' 'economic power cannot be easily transferred into any form of social capital' (Yu 2012: 237), given a male-dominated entertainment world and Chinese society in general. Nevertheless, Xu's boycott of the masculine theme as showcased in the two theme songs of *Duckweed* helped to propagate feminist ideas in the domain of media and popular culture in China.

In previous decades, even though the CCP promoted gender equality after it took over rule of mainland China, its gender policy not only failed to realize gender equality for contemporary Chinese women but also imposed a double burden on Chinese females as they had to contribute and sacrifice wholeheartedly to their country and to their family simultaneously. Acting as model workers in their work units, Chinese females, especially those who were married, did not enjoy equal status with their husbands in their households. The situation was exacerbated in the Opening Up period, when the overall political, social and cultural environment was more tolerant of moral deterioration. Many Chinese females have encountered and endured infidelity, physical abuse, emotional violence and even rape in their relationships.

Some recent scandalous events involving Chinese celebrities and stars have exposed this gender inequality and abuse in present-day Chinese society. On 11 August 2021, young celebrity singer Huo Zun's (霍尊) girlfriend, Chen Lu (陈露), published her relationship with Huo via her blog entry and accused

Huo of cheating, intimidation, threats and emotional violence in their nine-year romantic relationship. Chen's revelation was disastrous for Huo's career and caused him to withdraw from some popular reality show programmes after being publicly condemned for promiscuous behaviour. Huo's work studio verified his past relationship with Chen but denied Chen's accusations. Several months later, Huo confirmed to journalists that he and his family members had reported Chen's behaviour to the Shanghai police and that the case was under investigation.

Intimate partner violence (IPV) is the most common kind of domestic violence and a major public health problem. Around 35 per cent of the world's female population has experienced intimate partner violence or non-partner sexual violence in their lifetime. A report released by China Central Television (CCTV) shows that about 20 per cent of households experience domestic violence in China (Xu et al. 2022: 1). Moreover, 'there are offensive words used in the IPV reports that indicate misogyny and emotional, sexual, economic and psychological abuse' (Xu et al. 2022: 1–2). The deep-rooted culture of 'face' in China regards IPV as a private matter and people are inclined not to air their dirty laundry in public. As a result, IPV events in Chinese communities are often underreported.[1] However, owing to the spread of mobile internet and social media devices, IPV events involving celebrities have been brought to public awareness (Xu et al. 2022: 2). In real life, celebrity domestic violence incidents have garnered more attention and wider discussion, and 'Social media breaks the "gateway" barriers in traditional mass media, allowing the public to produce media content directly. Social networking platforms allow survivors to share their stories, promote these on behalf of survivors, and spread protection awareness' (Xu et al. 2022: 4). In the case of Huo Zun and Chen Lu, Huo's popularity attracted more attention to Chen's revelation; on the other hand, using the convenience brought by social media devices, Chen realized her role as a public opinion leader and women's rights defender and activist. Research also shows that the involvement of opinion leaders in IPV events has triggered an 'anti-silence effect', challenging traditional Chinese cultural factors such as face-saving and family shame that often prevent victims of IPV from exposing their encounters and suffering (Xu et al. 2022: 1–4).

Chen's accusation of Huo might be just the tip of the iceberg of the gender-related abuse and violence confronting females in a society still dominated by gender discrimination and male chauvinism, which has long been ignored and camouflaged by superficial and top-down propaganda claiming gender equality and social harmony. However, revelation of celebrities' IPV has attracted the attention of media and society at large to gender inequality and the emotional and physical abuse, violence and crimes in relationships that mainly victimize women and are rampant in current Chinese society. In December 2021, American-born Chinese pop singer-actor Wang Leehom's (王力宏) wife, Li Jinglei (李靓蕾), published an open letter reflecting on her divorce with Wang. In the letter, Li said that publishing this letter was the most difficult decision she had ever made in her life and she hoped that her sharing it would help those who were stuck in similar situations.

Li laid bare in her letter that since she married Wang, she had received non-stop suspicion, humiliation and emotional abuse from Wang and his family members. Li's revelation destroyed the fake image of a harmonious relationship between her and Wang and also the established public image of Wang. Wang had enjoyed extreme popularity in China as a pop singer and actor; he had been invited by CCTV to perform in the Spring Festival Gala several times, which reflected both the Chinese public and the government's perception of him as a flawless celebrity figure. Wang's public persona had been seamlessly manufactured by himself and his team as an energetic, passionate and patriotic young man via his songs, film roles and participation in public activities. In 2008, Wang contributed to the hit song of the Beijing Olympic Games, and in 2007, he starred as a jingoistic college student who organized the assassination of a Chinese traitor during the Anti-Japanese War in the film *Lust, Caution* (色戒) that was directed by Ang Li (李安). These appearances helped to build his positive public image as a nationalistic youth icon.

Wang's public persona formed a sharp contrast with the picture of an irresponsible and disloyal father and husband painted by his wife. In her letter, Li accused Wang of cheating in marriage and keeping various lovers and hiring prostitutes during their relationship; further, after she gave birth to three children at the expense of her own career, Wang acted irresponsibly to her and their children before he eventually abandoned them, forcing Li to divorce him. Before she decided to publish this letter, Li had endured Wang's betrayal and his family members' humiliation and emotional abuse to protect Wang's impeccable public image. However, after realizing that this was not the right way to protect her rights as an independent contemporary woman and to fulfill her social function as a public figure, Li decided to reveal her experiences in her marriage with Wang. She hoped to use her case to alert other Chinese women who were in similar situations, and to attract attention from the wider society and general public to the issue of IPV and its negative and disastrous effects on women. As pointed out by Marshall:

> While the celebrity is usually a complete stranger, and someone we are never likely to meet, nor ever truly know, the virtual intimacy created between celebrity and audience often has very real effects on the manner in which individuals negotiate the experience of their everyday lives. So, as well as being a consequential force within late capitalist Western liberal economies, celebrities are significant public entities responsible for structuring meaning, crystallizing ideologies, and offering contextually grounded maps for private individuals as they navigate contemporary conditions of existence. (Marshall 1997 cited in Andrews and Jackson 2001: 1–2)

Marshall's observation of the celebrity's function for ordinary people in the Western world also applies to the condition and environment of present-day China, in which 'celebrity coverage is a safe and seemingly harmless way into wider discussions about sexuality, morality and social roles . . . [and] popular star coverage appeals to the reader precisely because it can be used to engage in debates about fundamental moral issues, such as infidelity and the role of violence in society'. (Johansson 2006: 349 cited in Feasey 2008: 693)

At the beginning of her letter, Li wrote:

> Modern women are not like earlier women who did not have the right to receive education and therefore had no choice but to play the roles of wife and mother. We are very lucky to have the opportunity to receive higher education; we have the knowledge and ability to make a living and are also able to contribute to society. No matter whether one is a modern woman or a woman living in previous times, they choose to become a housewife and devote themselves wholeheartedly to their family. Though they do not get paid for doing so, they are still important supporters of their family as they are nannies, teachers, housekeepers, drivers, partners and personal assistants. The salary women should get from such a job should be added up from all these duties plus the cost to their opportunities for not working outside the home. This is the salary deserved by all the hardworking housewives, rather than being granted as a gift or alms. These women should not be constantly without financial independence and savings while their husband gets all the interests, rights and power; this will form an unequal relationship and put women in an inferior situation. Then, they will not have

the right to speak up even when their husbands have an affair or abuse them.
(李靓蕾长文原文内容王力宏和李靓蕾离婚原因是什么揭秘, 2021)

Li's confession sounds like a feminist manifesto from May Fourth times, when China's feminist thought and writing emerged and struck a chord with educated females. The reiteration of these feminist ideas seems to provide testimony to the failure of the cause of gender equality in mainland China. From another perspective, Li's confession explains why there emerged the phenomenon of 'leftover women' (剩女现象) in China, whereby aspirational young Chinese professional middle-class women who have higher education, high income and high intelligence choose to live a single and independent life: contemporary Chinese females shoulder too much in marriage and it is hard to achieve gender equality in their marriages.

Li's case may well represent millions of Chinese women's experiences of marriage. Similar experiences were also reflected in the plot of a 2016 TV drama hit entitled *The First Half of My Life* (我的前半生), which resonated with many Chinese female audiences. The show depicted the female lead's, Luo Zijun (罗子君), first half of life as comfortable but relying on the support of her husband; thus, when her husband had an extramarital affair, she was forced to divorce him and lost his economic support. Though the female protagonist in the show managed to live a better life through hard work after leaving her former husband, it is clear that not every woman has her good fortune in real life.

As Li continues in her letter:

I think this is a topic that our generation should reflect on. I have many housewife friends who do not have their own savings and income in their accounts, and they all feel embarrassed to use their husbands' money, act subserviently and live dependent on the whims of their husband when they ask them for money. They certainly dare not raise the topic of looking after their own parents. In our society, if women talk about money they are condemned as philistines or suspected of being gold diggers. For those women who have been unreservedly devoted to their family but were forced to divorce by their husbands without valid reasons, they feel nonplussed. Therefore, girls, we must prevent problems before they arise. I never thought I would experience all this, and you, too, might think it impossible! But it is certainly right to take precautions and plan ahead for yourselves and your children.
(李靓蕾长文原文内容王力宏和李靓蕾离婚原因是什么揭秘, 2021)

Li's revelation and the chord that it struck with ordinary people suggest that in the contemporary world, celebrity culture and influence demonstrate that 'the passion and frenzy of feeling that celebrity ignites and attaches itself to is part of a wider culture where sense and sensation, revelation and confession, outpouring and gossip have begun to shape the pulsating veins and arteries of everyday life' (Berlant 2011 cited in Redmond 2019: 58). Further, Li's case shows that 'the star and celebrity confession is ideological and discursive, bound up with identity politics, power relationships, and the political economy' (Redmond 2008: 111).

Li's words exposed the hardships and voice of those Chinese females who lost themselves, their career, their independence and their dignity in their marriage, and she became a spokesperson for women who wanted to defend their rights and self-esteem. While fulfilling her social function as a public figure, Li turned herself into a popular activist defending female rights and dignity.

Back in 2018, a young Shanghainese actress, Shen Lijun (沈丽君), took her own life after suffering from cancer and cheating and IPV from her husband. While she was still popular, Shen quit the entertainment scene after getting married and raising two kids. In her posthumous paper, Shen revealed that during her marriage that lasted for eight years, she endured cheating, betrayal and emotional and physical violence from her husband. She could not bear it any longer and chose to end her own life after being diagnosed with late-stage cancer. Given that Shen was not a top star, her tragedy did not attract much attention from the media and the public regarding protecting women's rights and well-being in marriage. Even less did it trigger the Chinese version of the #MeToo movement (米兔运动), as Chinese female rights defenders and activists face a much harsher environment in China. Government restrictions and control of the media have limited their capacity to build comparable momentum to activists abroad.

Though a young celebrity's death did not raise much awareness of the disturbing circumstances of many Chinese females, the plight of a middle-aged rural woman who was abducted elevated the public's attention towards Chinese women's rights to an unprecedented level. In early 2022, a Chinese netizen published a self-media report that revealed the sad story of a Chinese village woman with schizophrenia who had been abducted and sold to a man in a village in Xuzhou, Jiangsu Province. The woman was forced into marriage with the man and gave birth to eight of his children. Human trafficking and the abduction of women and children are open secrets caused by the serious gender imbalance, particularly in the countryside, which has led to many poor Chinese male farmers, young and old, failing to find a wife. As a solution, many of them buy wives from human traffickers and bribe local government officials to issue marriage certificates to them and these women. This kind of violation of women is widespread in China's underdeveloped countryside, where local government officers connive with human traffickers to trample women's rights in exchange for unlawful income. The Chinese government limits media reporting of sensitive issues such as human trafficking and so the public rarely reads in-depth coverage of human trafficking via mainstream media outlets.

Thanks to the emergence and rapid development of self-media platforms, reports revolving around sensitive and taboo topics have become hot topics of civil and human rights discussions among the Chinese. Shocking images and videos of the abducted woman, who was shackled by her neck and lived in a deserted room, immediately touched millions of Chinese netizens, who were eager to read follow-up reports and request an explanation from the local government. The report also triggered heated and intensive debates and criticism among the Chinese public regarding women's rights in contemporary China, corruption of local government officials and human rights concerns. Given the enormous attention and discussion prompted by the report, both freelance journalists and the local government in Xuzhou conducted investigations into the woman's case; however, the Chinese public could not accept the outcome of the government's investigation, which held that the woman had been formally married to her captor and she might have had a mental disorder before she was sold to him. The government's perfunctory conclusions fuelled irritation among Chinese people and compelled them to contemplate the reality of human rights in current-day China. Many netizens expressed that they worried about themselves and their family members who might encounter a similar fate, which led them to question the government's ability to guarantee the safety of its citizens and further to question the government's reputation and legitimacy to rule the country.

Back to Li's letter, in which she mentioned that contemporary Chinese females are judged as philistines or labelled as gold diggers if they discuss money with their partners or marry a rich man. Taking female celebrities and stars as examples, they would be first judged as money-chasers if they married a rich businessman, a 'rich second generation' or married into a wealthy family. Mainland Chinese actress Liu Tao (刘涛) married a rich Beijing businessman in 2007; in 2008 the couple held a grand wedding ceremony and Liu was described as a 'Cinderella' who married into a wealthy family. In 2010, mainland actress Che Xiao (车晓) married the richest man of Shanxi Province and the couple divorced in 2012. Che became more famous for her divorce than her acting, as she was treated by media as a typical gold digger who had demanded 300 million yuan in compensation from her husband – claims denied by Che in subsequent interviews.

In 2010, Taiwanese actress Xu Xiyuan (徐熙媛, nicknamed 'Big S') married a mainland 'rich second generation', Wang Xiaofei (汪小菲), after a lightning-quick courtship. Wang was five years her junior, and the couple divorced in 2021. Though during their marriage, the couple had two kids and flaunted their happy life constantly to the public, people seemed more willing to believe that Xu married Wang for his rich family background. Some media even gloated over Wang's misfortune when his family business faced huge difficulties and mocked Xu for marrying a 'fake rich second generation'. Similarly, Taiwanese celebrities Wu Peici (吴佩慈) and An Yixuan (安以轩) both married rich mainland businessmen and were labelled as Taiwanese gold diggers by the mainland media. When their husbands' businesses encountered setbacks, the media and netizens univocally took pleasure in these gold digger celebrities' misfortunes.

The media and public's reaction to these female stars' misfortune reflects a deep-rooted conception of and discrimination against Chinese females that assumes women are dependent on men and rely on men for material satisfaction. This established contempt and bias towards females have been reinforced in recent times as mainstream media and the public assume that 'leftover women' are left in the marriage market because they harbour unrealistically high expectations of their future husbands. Like female celebrities and stars, the so-called leftover women are those professional and financially independent women who have career aspirations and enjoy quality lifestyles; thus, they bravely choose to live a single life and compete with men in the career field. Through their love and marriage choices, these women show that they would not marry for money and material enjoyment; they can rely on themselves to satisfy all their needs.

Several years after her marriage, Liu Tao's husband went bankrupt and encountered mental health issues. Liu came back to the entertainment circle after giving birth to two kids to repay her husband's debts. In several interviews, Liu confessed how anxious she was about her husband and the family's situation and how hard she worked to save money. Eventually, she paid off all the debts and her husband also recovered from his setback and mental problems; the whole family resumed a happy life. Liu's commitment to her family was praised far and wide in the entertainment world and by the general audience. Liu was applauded and admired as a typical good woman of China who sacrificed for her husband and family without any complaints, and she subsequently played many virtuous wife or good woman roles in TV drama shows, which cashed in on her real-life experiences. Here, the extreme popularity gained by Liu among the audience proves that celebrities and stars 'rely on the confessional to authenticate, validate, humanise, resurrect, extend and enrich their star and celebrity identities. Stars and celebrities confess, and in so doing confirm their status as truthful, emotive, experiential beings who as devotional fans we can invest in' (Redmond 2008: 110).

Liu's devotion to her family changed her original persona as a Cinderella and gold digger and won her respect; however, from another perspective, her popularity and reputation as a good wife and wise mother reflect how contemporary Chinese women are judged against traditional Chinese thinking, gender and behavioural rules and moral bindings. In other words, Liu's achievements as a stereotypical virtuous Chinese woman strengthen traditional and conservative expectations of Chinese females, which might serve as obstacles on the path to the rights and enjoyment of Chinese women. In Xu Xiyuan's case, she divorced Wang Xiaofei in 2021 after a marriage that had lasted for more than a decade and immediately entered into another flash marriage; this time her husband is a former Korean singer who is not young or rich at all. Xu's choice resembles that of many Chinese women today, who do not want to be trapped in an unfruitful marriage and are courageous enough to listen to the voice deep in their hearts.

There is enormous gossip involving extramarital affairs, IPV and marriage breakup between Xu, Wang and Xu's new husband. Celebrity revelation, gossip and scandals generate social debates among Chinese audiences, which increases Chinese people's opportunity and eagerness to participate in discussions about gender relations and women's rights. According to

Redmond (2019: 59–60), celebrities' 'confession and its associated forms of gossip are "female" centred' because of the position of 'women within patriarchal frames that limit their access to, and involvement with, the more serious, more "rational" public world' (Redmond 2019: 59–60). Moreover, as Feasey (2008: 692) puts it, 'celebrity gossip can be understood as a powerful feminine discourse and as a way of connecting like-minded young women'; 'the discussion about celebrity . . . can serve a normative function, in that a sense of togetherness is established' (Johanson 2006: 349 cited in Feasey 2008: 692). The social function of celebrity suggests that 'gossip is . . . an important social process, through which relationships, identity, and social and cultural norms are debated, evaluated, modified and shared' (Turner 2004: 24 cited in Feasey 2008: 692).

In Li Jinglei's open letter, she also criticized powerful people including celebrities and stars, such as her husband Wang Leehom, who, she said, should not fabricate their public image through media devices, thereby misinforming the public and further deforming social values. Li explained her motives in releasing her experiences in her letter:

> I have decided to speak up because I do not want other women to experience what I have experienced. I also think this world needs more reflection. For ages, powerful people have manipulated media and the media manipulate the public, which leads to the distortion of societal values as the public's thoughts are controlled. I hope in the future those powerful people will be prohibited from maintaining their public image and controlling public opinion through marketing. Thus, the public will know the truth of public figures. I feel I have the social responsibility to ensure that other people will not tread in my footsteps without knowing my experiences.
> (李靓蕾长文原文内容王力宏和李靓蕾离婚原因是什么揭秘, 2021)

It is common knowledge nowadays that stars and their marketing teams use various devices and opportunities to manufacture and maintain their charismatic and positive public personae. During this process, false and pretentious characters and personal life events are produced to create upbeat public images, which mislead the audience and fans and sometimes even harm other people's interests and reputations. In the case of Wang Leehom and Li Jinglei, to sustain his own healthy public persona, Wang tried to discredit Li's public image. He might easily have achieved this if Li did not speak up, given that he is a super star and Li is only a public figure because of Wang's influence. In other words, counting on their popularity and superior social impact, celebrities and stars are the leading voice in the media environment and in society. However, in Wang's case, his own denials of Li's indictment, together with his father's rebuffing of Li's accusation – in which he claimed that Li forced Wang to marry her because she was pregnant with his child and Li asked for a huge allowance after the divorce – unexpectedly furthered public impressions of Wang as irresponsible, consequently making Li's revelation more credible and her resistance as a female rights supporter more powerful.

In the tension between idol worship and supporting women's rights, the public prioritize defending of women's rights. Research shows:

> The public in China has become concerned about IPV events and encourages victims to seek legal help. . . . The vast majority of netizens hate perpetrators and have the attitude that perpetrators should be punished. Furthermore, the public believes that IPV is illegal and supports punishing perpetrators through legal means. People provided, affirmed and encouraged the victims' disclosure of domestic violence, which expands the cognitive scope of IPV. (Xu et al. 2022: 20)

Li's revelation of her IPV experiences demonstrates that in the contemporary Chinese world of entertainment, stars initiate reflection and debate of civil and human rights issues, including women's rights, and trigger women's rights-defence activities and campaigns. There might be different reasons that pushed Chen and Li to expose Huo and Wang's immoral conduct in their relationships, and it is difficult to discern what exactly happened between them. However, it is apparent that Chinese celebrities and stars have become targets of gender-related abuse and violence and placed in the limelight, which has prompted more attention from the public towards rights-defending actions and movements of contemporary Chinese women. In the comparatively conservative Sinophone cultural sphere, women need courage to speak up for themselves and their peers, particularly those women who accuse their celebrity and star partners or their powerful partners in the political realm (in the case of Peng Shuai). These women are highly likely to face cyberbullying by the fans of those star figures; however, their voices have started to be heard and in the long term this might change the media ecology and the public opinion in the online environment.

Besides maltreatment, cheating, abuse and violence against females, crimes committed against women are also exposed more often in the entertainment domain, revealing celebrities and stars to be at the epicentre of moral decadence and social instability. In recent years, Chinese celebrities and stars have frequently been enlisted as negative examples by the government to tighten their control over people's morality, particularly over the teenager and youth cohorts. For example, Chinese president Xi Jinping's administration singled out the 'Nancy Boy' trend in the entertainment industry and sought to clean up the physical looks of performers, including forbidding tattoos from being shown along with earrings on men.

Regulations were announced in 2019 that strive to promote 'healthy cultural education', according to the regulators. Kris Wu is a young Canada-based singer-actor who emerged as China's leading Nancy Boy figure, or 'young fresh meat' (小鲜肉), which is a phrase used to describe pretty male pop or screen idols. In July 2021, Wu was accused of sexually assaulting and raping several teenage girls after getting them drunk or in a state of unconsciousness. Du Meizhu (都美竹), a teenage girl who was Wu's fan, revealed in a Weibo post that she was raped by Wu while inebriated when she was still a minor. According to Du, other underage girls had been ravished by Wu in similar ways (都美竹再爆料吴亦凡信息量大, 2021). Though Wu denied Du's allegations, the Beijing Public Security Bureau launched an investigation into the potential sex crimes, and Wu was arrested in August 2021. This caused huge damage to Wu's career and reputation. World-class brands such as Bulgari and Lancôme dumped him as a brand ambassador or halted remaining endorsement contracts. Based on the police's investigation, Wu was sentenced to eleven years in jail in 2022.

Wu was one of the top stars in China's entertainment circle to have fallen from grace because of crimes against women. Though there were cases that have been reported and confirmed regarding single male stars hiring prostitutes, the public's attitude towards these cases is comparatively open and tolerant. While prostituting is banned in China by the government, it seems to occupy a grey area if the whore-goer is not in a married relationship. However, rape is a serious crime against women, especially when involving the doping or enticement of underaged women, which will certainly generate anger and concern among the public. When a male celebrity or star uses their public persona, social resources and power to take advantage of his young female fans, this creates a complex condition in which gender, media and power elements are entangled in an imbalanced and conflicting way. From Du's perspective, she was the underdog in these struggles with Wu, as Wu held more media assets and power in the entertainment world. He also had more financial power, which, according to Du, he used to bribe his close friends to slander her and discredit her accusations. Despite all of this, Du's revelation showed that she had the courage to speak up for herself and other victims, even if she knew she might lose the battle against Wu. It is common knowledge that many rape victims are reluctant to report and publicize their misfortune because it engenders so much psychological suffering and there is still such stigma attached to rape.

In Wu's case, adoring young Chinese fans attempted to justify their excessive support by referring to the nature of fandom. They argued that being a fan, by definition, means fanatic and unconditional support for the object of fandom (Yang 2009: 537). Thus, they demonstrated extreme despising and hatred towards Du's revelations and tried hard to destroy Du's public image in order to protect their own idol, Wu. Wu's fans' irrational admiration of him illustrates that 'Asian fandom is star-centric, not character-centric' and 'Chinese fandom is tied to the conventions of pan-Asian stardom' (Chin 2007: 216). As scholars have noted, Asian fans constantly return to the figure of the star as the object of adoration instead of a particular film work or genre. Even within the sphere of the internet, on websites and forums, Asian fans are mostly geared towards an actor rather than a film (Chin 2007; Weiss 2013).

Though her revelations attracted enormous cyberbullying from Wu's fans, Du's allegations triggered debate on China's #MeToo movement and celebrity culture. Wu's case has been regarded by some cultural critics as part of a broader movement in China similar to the #MeToo movement in the United States, where influential entertainment industry figures were called, humiliated and sometimes indicted for previous conduct supposed to be offensive or manipulative (Kris Wu faces rape charges 2021). The Chinese version of the #MeToo movement reached a peak in 2018, when a Beijing-based screenwriter, Zhou Xiaoxuan (周晓璇), alleged that she had been sexually assaulted by Zhu Jun (朱军), a veteran television host from CCTV. Zhou reported the incident to the police and took her case to court. However, the court rebuffed her claims against Zhu because of inadequate proof; Zhu denied all charges. Zhou's case can be compared with counterparts in Western societies, given that 'misogyny and domestic violence are global phenomena' (Xu et al. 2022: 18). In Britain, for example, there have been a significant number of media reports in recent years concerning accusations of sexual assaults perpetrated by Premier League footballers; however, these stories have failed to dent the careers of the individuals involved. Low conviction rates indicate the 'failure of both the legal system and society at large to tackle sexual violence' (Gies 2011: 349).

Though Zhou lost the lawsuit against Zhu, her revelations gained enormous attention from the public. They led to a peak in China's #MeToo movement and Zhou herself has become a leading advocate of this movement, which she has helped to promote by taking advantage of new technologies to connect with other survivors of sexual assault and share their stories on social media (Xu et al. 2022: 18). However, the Chinese version of the #MeToo movement failed to build up a comparable momentum to those elsewhere. Chinese society is still firmly dominated by males and elements of Confucian thought that discipline and constrain women. A tradition of Chinese females and feminists to fight for their rights is lacking, added to the government's censorship and control of the media coverage of controversial and sensitive topics.

Protecting women's rights was at the top of the agenda for the CCP government when it took over the rule of mainland China. It banned prostitution and promoted female model workers; however, sometimes these measures backfired, as some prostitutes chose their job of their own accord, and pushing women to perform similarly to men in the workforce increased their burdens because they also shouldered heavy duties in households. Unfortunately, today, there is no sign that the CCP government is prioritizing women's rights in any real sense; for example, sexual harassment and abuse are still rampant in China's officialdom and government organizations across all levels. Rather than supporting China's own #MeToo movement, the official mouthpiece newspaper *Global Times* (环球时报) claimed that foreign countries used the #MeToo movement to 'tear Chinese society apart' and tried to blame women's rights-defending activities and campaigns such as the #MeToo movement on political interference from foreign governments (Lan 2021). This allegation of the *Global Times* raised the timely women's rights-defence movements in China to the level of a major national issue. This confused the public and demonstrated that the Chinese government is afraid of its people campaigning to protect their rights because it might ignite people's fervour to campaign for other rights such as suffrage and right of free assembly. It is widely observed that the current Chinese government is strengthening its authoritarian rule, which has been shown through its forceful locking down of China's biggest and most energetic city, Shanghai, to control the Covid pandemic and maintain its image. To some degree, the censored #MeToo movement in China demonstrates to the world how China's authoritarian rule works and suppresses the rights of its people.

Apart from reflecting the physical and emotional abuse and violence in relationships, celebrities and stars became the focus of other women rights issues such as reproductive rights. For example, acclaimed Chinese dancer Yang Liping (杨丽萍) published a vlog in which she was having hotpot in a room decorated with many fresh flowers. Yang is somewhat of an emblem of unworldly people and life in contemporary China given the unusual lifestyle she follows: her life has been dedicated to her dancing career and she remains single and without children. Yang's public image is like a white lotus flower because of her transcendence and purity; she is romantic, beautiful and otherworldly. Yang sometimes posts photos via her social media accounts showing her having tea in her private gardens with birds standing on her shoulders, which resembles the lifestyle of recluses in ancient China who were cut off from the outside world. Yang's video post was mocked by one netizen who published a comment on Yang's blog page:

> The biggest failure of a woman is that she does not have a child. It simply lies to say that she moves her own way. How come you look like you are in your thirties when you are one hundred years old? You cannot stand the wear and tear of time. When you are in your nineties, you will not enjoy family happiness as you do not have children and grandchildren. (杨丽萍‘不生孩子’被群嘲：女性的婚姻与生育都应是自由的, 2020)

This netizen's comment on Yang's lifestyle struck a chord with many netizens and received 10,000 'likes' in a very short time, becoming the top trending topic on WeChat and triggering hot debate among millions of people.

In the meantime, other female celebrities and stars have started to share their own comments on women's lifestyles and rights and tear into those advocates of a so-called perfect life of a woman. They consider that it has long been outmoded to judge a woman's life using marriage and childbirth as criteria. Li Ruotong (李若彤), a Hong Kong-based actress, shares her opinion:

> As a single and mature female, I receive similar questions and comments every day via social media platforms such as why are you still unmarried? And I want to say why I must get married? Perhaps I have not met the right guy at the correct time, and in my opinion remaining single is better than marrying a wrong person and leading an unhappy life. So those people who are viewing this blog post, no matter whether you are a man or a woman, I hope you would not make a careless decision for your life due to age or other people's opinion, and one must learn to respect other people's decisions, because that is other people's life. (杨丽萍'不生孩子'被群嘲：女性的婚姻与生育都应是自由的, 2020)

Popular mainland actress Qi Wei (戚薇) posted: 'the biggest failure of a person is: still trying to define our women up until today, and still taking children and grandchildren as the only criteria by which to judge the success of a woman's life'. Singer Li Na (厉娜) comments:

> I can choose to give birth because I want to do it, I can choose not to give birth because I have the right to make a decision for myself. Shut up and live your own life, because those are the basic qualities of a human being. Women just need to live the life they want and do not need to care about any definitions bestowed by others. (杨丽萍'不生孩子'被群嘲：女性的婚姻与生育都应是自由的, 2020)

Chen Shu (陈数), one of China's top female stars, also published comments in which she denies that a woman's value is to give birth to children. Yang Liping gave her own response to netizens' comments:

> A little ant is also my child, and my dancing performances are also my daughters . . . some people's life is for keeping the family line, some people's is enjoyment, experience and observation. I am an observer of life. I came to the world to watch how a tree grows, how a river flows, how clouds float, and how manna condenses. (杨丽萍'不生孩子'被群嘲：女性的婚姻与生育都应是自由的, 2020)

Undoubtedly, the widespread debate about what makes a perfect life journey for a woman has revealed that contemporary Chinese females' understanding of marriage, childbirth, reproductive rights and the social function of women has changed and diversified. Marriage and childbirth have acted as social and moral institutions that have bound Chinese women from time immemorial. Many women confront huge familial and social pressure, and some are forced to make choices that are against their own will.

Famous women such as celebrities and stars bear even more stress as they are public figures and shoulder a social function. Thus, these women who have social influence speak up for freedom in marriage and childbirth and provide universal education about gender equality, which helps to reach social consensus on these issues and prevent groundless accusations and moral blackmail regarding women's free choices. Further, freedom in marriage and childbirth are protected by laws including the Constitution and the Marriage Law; therefore, it is against the law to interfere in these kinds of rights of women. Celebrities' and stars' statements and attitudes towards reproductive rights particularly and women's rights generally contribute to the realization of the gender equality in today's China, which to a certain degree is still dominated by men and gender inequality (杨丽萍'不生孩子'被群嘲：女性的婚姻与生育都应是自由的, 2020).

Some open-minded and avant-garde Chinese female celebrities and stars further advocate the sexual freedom of women, which is another independent women's right that deserves to be safeguarded and fought for. The famous high-born 'ruffian' Hong Huang's (洪晃)[2] attitudes and understanding towards sex serve as an alternative and correction to the established sexual concepts of many Chinese women, in particular those older generation women, who safeguard their body and chastity from being 'contaminated' and taken advantage of by men before marriage. In China, even in the modern-day social context, if women have premarital or extramarital sex with men, they are deemed as cheap, dissolute and taken advantage of by men. This is very much in line with the patriarchal and conventional codes of Chinese ethics, which put Chinese women in a passive, inferior and disadvantaged position in their relationship with men. However, Hong Huang believes that the sexual bond between a man and woman is a purely equal, fair and reciprocal association, in which men and women enjoy and enrich each other. According to Hong Huang, lovemaking is a good way to detect a man's nature – to see, for example, if he is good and honest, gentle, fair and romantic. Hong Huang believes that the traditional Chinese moral principles truly misguide women as they instruct them not to have sex before marriage despite the fact that a man's quality and nature are most likely to be exposed through the act of lovemaking.

In Hong Huang's opinion, for women to offer their beauty and body for men to consume is a disrespectful and unwise idea. Here, Hong's opinion concurs with that of Banyard as he argued that 'capitalism has triumphed "selling" feminism back to us in the forms of playboy motifs and products; women's willingness to engage in their own commercialisation as objects' (Banyard 2010 cited in Savigny and Warner 2015: 15).

Hong advises women that they should consume their own beauty and youth, date as much as they want and sleep with men as much as they like. In other words, they should 'consume' men instead of being 'consumed' by men. Hong's non-conformist language and behaviour have given her a rebellious, vulgar and feminist streak, which has won her both acclaim and criticism from cultural and social critics and the general public. Hong Huang's high-born background and celebrity identity win her much attention and debate regarding her lifestyle and philosophy as an avant-garde female of modern-day China. She advances Chinese feminism as a discursive force in its challenge to the still-male-dominated Chinese society. Through adopting a rational and confident stance in her understanding of sex, Hong Huang sets up a fresh, innovative and progressive image for the contemporary Chinese female. Relying on her unique and charismatic temperament, her intelligent and humorous style of conversation, and her independent and courageous thinking, Hong Huang moulds herself into a spokesperson for contemporary China's 'non-utilitarian' feminism.

Muzi Mei (木子美)[3] is another advocate of women's sexual freedom. In some Chinese people's eyes, she is a symbol of sexual love and 'shamelessness'; in others, she is a representative of moral defiance and a new lifestyle. Muzi Mei is a female internet writer who publishes her own sexual experiences in her blog (www.blogchina.net), which is a daily diary of her sexual encounters and other activities. After being published as a book in 2004 under the title *Diary of Sexual Love* (性爱日记), her private website became one of the most popular in China.[4] Muzi and her sexual diaries attracted huge attention from the media. Elaine Jeffreys (2006: 6) has remarked on similar phenomena: 'Media reports often imply that Chinese women are finally embracing Western-style sexual liberation, as evidenced by publications detailing the "real-life" casual sexual adventurism of young, unmarried women.'

Muzi can be regarded as one of China's best-known first-generation internet celebrities, and her case encompasses a variety of discourses about contemporary celebrity culture. In contrast to the traditional concept of famous people who reach outstanding achievements in their respective fields, such as well-known scientists, sportspersons and actors, Muzi's celebrity status has been attained in an unconventional way, or through a self-made course that is realized through being eccentric, or even notorious. Blogs have made celebrities like Muzi a possibility, as individuals can publicize their life, ideas and even once-private matters in a more unrestricted manner. Utilizing a blog for its audience reach, Muzi self-promotes her trifles of lifestyle and persona as independent, liberal, self-directed, hedonistic and sex-indulged. Muzi's success and her attainment of celebrity status largely come from her successful marketing of herself via the new mass media platform as a 'loose woman', a 'body writer', a self-centred and open-minded contemporary female, and a pleasure-seeking sex-addict.

Similar to Hong Huang's idea of 'consuming' men, Muzi proposes a new sex concept, 'consoled by others' ('他慰', which is derived from '自慰'), in one of her early novellas. She impresses that she represents 'Generation X', and the idea of being 'consoled by others' is a kind of female hedonism (*Diary of Sexual Love*, chapter 10). Both Hong Huang's notion of 'consuming' men and Muzi's notion of being 'consoled by others' foreground women as the centre and 'agent' of sex. This bears a feminist imprint, even though neither writer claims to be a feminist. Again, like Hong Huang, who makes risqué jokes that harass, mock and embarrass her male friends and colleagues, Muzi reverses the roles of men and women regarding sexual matters by commenting on men's sexual skills and publicizing their identity, which not only humiliates them but also scares them. Consequently, Muzi successfully transforms the timid and 'restrained' Chinese female into a 'debauched' and intimidating woman. Her writing is a springboard for Chinese women's conversion from compliant and apathetic recipients of sex to brusque commanders of it.

Using her sex blogs, Muzi Mei's writing also serves as a signifier of a mounting individualism and a challenge to an all-controlling state, mainly through her apparent defiance of media censorship and previous constraints on public expressions of sexuality (Jeffreys and Edwards 2010: 12–13). There are arguments that reveal 'how celebrity culture subsidizes the social courses through which human relationships, identity and cultural norms are created and deliberated' (Marshall 1997; Jeffreys and Edwards 2010), and also demonstrate that celebrity culture and the celebrity industry herald 'a new mode of media operation and different ways of informing and shaping a general public' (Jeffreys and Edwards 2010: 7). In the case of Muzi Mei, her sex blog diaries 'create new venues for individuals to exercise cultural citizenship' as the internet discussions that were sparked by her sex blogs serve as evidence of 'collective social action and community building by justifying certain conceptions of "rights"' (Jeffreys and Edwards 2010: 13–14).

Chinese *wanghong* as public activists

The vernacular term in China for internet celebrities is *wanghong* (网红). According to Abidin (2018: 2–3), it 'translates to "red on the internet" with the colour red signifying popularity, and broadly refers to highly prolific internet users who are effective conduits for channelling online retail businesses or social media advertising'. The *wanghong* gains celebrity status not for any kind of verifiable talent but for their particular capacity to attract attention on the internet. Varieties of Chinese *wanghong* have garnered enormous popularity among Chinese internet users. Some sell and promote clothing and commodities via their live-streaming sessions; others share scenes from their family life, career experiences or tips for make-up; and some big eaters simply video themselves eating meals, which can easily attract millions of views. Another discernible feature of the Chinese *wanghong* phenomenon is that urban people are eager to watch the daily routines of farmers living in the impoverished countryside, including working in the fields and other household tasks. One reason for this might be that viewing the living conditions in the comparatively less affluent countryside provides satisfaction to the city dwellers who enjoy a materially comfortable life.

Though the Chinese *wanghong* economy mainly manufactures internet celebrities who are concerned only with their own interests and profit, some use the internet and social media outlets to promote civic and human rights and turn themselves into public activists. An interesting and thought-provoking case of Chinese *wanghong*, Li Jiaqi (李佳琦)[1] took place around 4 June 2022, which marked the 33rd anniversary of the brutal crackdown on the Tiananmen democratic demonstration led by China's college students. In the years after the 4th June demonstration, the Chinese government tried their best to conceal the truth of the event and prevent younger generations of Chinese people from knowing anything about the event. In Chinese middle school and university textbooks, the demonstration was briefly described as a riot mobilized and triggered by overseas anti-Chinese-government forces. Film, TV and media productions must avoid this sensitive topic if they want to be released in mainland China.

Every year, when the 4th June anniversary is approaching, the Chinese government is highly vigilant against the movement of political activists, particularly those 'Tiananmen Mothers' who lost their children during the violent crackdown that happened on the 4th of June 1989. During this period, these people might be put under residential surveillance in case they organize public demonstrations or other anti-government campaigns that are viewed by the CCP as threatening to the stability of its rule. Coincidentally, during this period in 2022, Chinese web influencer Li Jiaqi promoted a tank-shaped ice cream cake during his live-streaming session. His live stream was cut and his live site was banned immediately. Tanks are iconic of the 4th June crackdown as the People's Liberation Army drove into Tiananmen Square in tanks as many brave students and Beijing city residents tried to block their advance. Moreover, these confrontations between the students and residents and the soldiers led to combat and possibly thousands of civilian casualties. Therefore, the appearance of the tank-shaped ice cream cake during the live-streaming of *wanghong* Li Jiaqi at this sensitive time brought trouble to him as the CCP government swiftly blocked the tank image before it could reach more web users.

The followers and fans of web influencers and *wanghong* are chiefly young generations of Chinese people who lack even basic knowledge of the 4th June incident, thanks to the successful brainwashing and obscuring of the event by the CCP propaganda machines; the tank image actually would not attract their attention. However, the closing of Li Jiaqi's live room and the reporting surrounding it instead stimulated their curiosity about why Li's live room was banned by the government. As a result, they came to know about the 4th June demonstration and the brutal clampdown on it, which inspired their passion to explore the tragic event further. The government probably would not have thought that its ban on Li's live room would lead to increasing attention towards the 4th June event, putting the party in a more delicate situation (李佳琦直播被封 促90后找真相 中共陷尴尬, 2022).

Obviously in Li's case, he became 'unexpected collateral damage' (躺枪) under the extreme surveillance and monitoring of the Chinese public by the authoritarian CCP regime. Li's live-stream sessions focus on teaching viewers make-up skills and promoting cosmetics; however, other web influencers have achieved celebrity status by fashioning themselves into public activists. One example is the Chinese freelance reporter Chen Qiushi (陈秋实), who actively participated in the Anti-Extradition Law Amendment Bill Movement (Anti-ELAB Movement) in Hong Kong in 2019. In August 2019, Chen arrived in Hong Kong as a tourist and participated in the gathering and demonstration organized by the Hong Kong pro-democracy camp at Victoria Gardens. At this, he called for the Hong Kong people to explain what was happening in Hong Kong to the mainland public. Further, Chen shared what he had seen and heard in Hong Kong on his Sina Blog, and he was urged by the public security agency to go back to the mainland only three days after he arrived in Hong Kong. Later in August 2019, Chen's login on Sina Blog was cancelled, and in October, his TikTok account was cancelled. In December, Chen's WeChat official account was cancelled because it 'spread negative rumours' and other contents that were against the law. From October, Chen started to open accounts on Twitter and YouTube to publish news of his current situation and commentary. As everyone knows, Twitter has long been banned in mainland China. In recent years, Twitter has become a gathering place for many Chinese political dissidents, human rights activists and overseas Chinese, who want to discuss those topics that have been censored and banned in mainland China (中国活动人士和异见者为何在Twitter上遭压制, 2023)

On 23 January 2020, when Wuhan and several other cities in Hubei Province were under lockdown because of the Covid-19 pandemic, Chen went to Wuhan to investigate. On his second day in Wuhan, Chen made some field visits to local hospitals to record the impact of Covid-19. During Chen's short stay in Wuhan, he published videos recording his experiences almost on a daily basis, which revealed the chaotic and disastrous situation in Wuhan, including that numerous Covid-19 patients suffered and died owing to a shortage of medical resources. In his 24 January video published on his YouTube channel, Chen said:

> Today is the new year's eve according to the Chinese lunar calendar, and it is not my business to know where Xi Jinping is, but Chen Qiushi is here in Wuhan, and I want to face this disastrous situation alongside the Wuhan residents.

Further, Chen commented:

> I wish people could let each other know the truth about the COVID-19 virus, as covering up the truth and the disastrous situation during the SARS pandemic caused enormous loss of human life and I do not want this to happen again.

At the end of this video, Chen called for help from the Western developed world:

> I beg you to help China and Wuhan. Though in the past years the Chinese government has swaggered nonstop in the international arena, that does not represent the voice and wishes of the entire Chinese population. I know that even when you help China this time, the Chinese government will accuse you of being 'overseas anti-Chinese forces', but that is how the Chinese government is. However, the millions of Chinese people are innocent. In the past decades, Chinese people have endured too much misery and tribulation, so it is time to make changes. (陈秋实：我和武汉人民共同进退, 2020)

In his YouTube video post published on 31 January, Chen openly questioned the official count of people who had passed away because of the Covid-19 virus. He suspected it was much lower than the actual number because of what he had seen and heard in Wuhan (勇敢真实的声音非常重要: 陈秋实大年初八中午武汉总结播报, 2020). In his YouTube video posts, Chen spoke up for Chinese people. He openly criticized the dereliction of duty on the part of the Chinese government and the Chinese president Xi Jinping, alleging that they covered up the truth of the pandemic to the Chinese people and the world, and avoided reporting the suffering and tribulations of the Wuhan residents. Moreover, Chen revealed the truth that the Chinese government cannot represent its people, which indicates that the CCP government had lost the respect, trust and loyalty of its people. Also, Chen pointed out the fact that to save its own face, the Chinese government would not seek help from the Western world; it would rather sacrifice the lives of its people (陈秋实：我和武汉人民共同进退, 2020).

In response to his criticism of the government in his video posts, Chen was detained by the public security agency on 6 February 2020. His mother confirmed his arrest on his YouTube channel. Chen disappeared from Wuhan. On 17 September 2020, Chen's close friend Xu Xiaodong (徐晓冬) released news of Chen in his live stream, during which Xu verified that in the past few months Chen's physical and mental health had been okay, and he had left Wuhan. Because there was no evidence that Chen had conducted any behaviour that involved inciting subversion of state power, there would be no prosecution. On 29 March 2021, Xu revealed that Chen had started to gain some freedom and was allowed to frequent areas close to his home. He could go to see the doctor and read news reports. However, because of the 'protection' of relevant government organs, Chen still could not communicate with the outside world. Also, there were several secret agents conducting patrols and surveillance out of his apartment, and there was an unidentified person in his apartment who monitored his movements.

After he disappeared for almost 600 days during the Covid-19 pandemic, Chen released a video post in February 2022, which was a special post in memory of doctor Li Wenliang (李文亮),[2] the whistle-blower of the Covid-19 virus who later died from it himself. In this video post, Chen commented:

On the day that doctor Li Wenliang passed away, I was arrested. During the following months of interrogations, I was repeatedly told by the police that: first, I was guilty because I exposed those scandals of China to the rest of the world; second, under the rule of the Chinese government and the CCP, China achieved huge success in the battle against the COVID-19 pandemic; third, the Americans totally failed in their battle with the virus because more than a million American people died from it, and the virus might even have been manufactured by an American military base . . .

During the past one or two months, China has spent an enormous amount of money on producing an extremely bad Spring Festival evening gala; spent a huge amount of money maintaining a soccer team that is good at losing games; and spent even more money on holding the Winter Olympic Games. For those athletes coming from all over the world, it doesn't matter whether you can ski, provided you come you will get a big gift pack that is worth thousands of yuan . . . China is really rich. However, if China is that rich, why won't it spend some money on a monument for doctor Li Wenliang? It is not because of lack of money, it is because it does not want to . . .

I wonder, after ten years, how much memory about doctor Li Wenliang will still exist and circulate on China's internet? . . . and if there is no narrative about doctor Li Wenliang in China's history textbooks, is China still a country that respects history?
(李文亮如果不能写进历史教科书中国还是个尊重历史的国家吗? 2022)

At the end of this video post, Chen encouraged his audiences to remember doctor Li Wenliang and said that his death should wake Chinese people up to their rights and duties to fight for freedom of speech and media.

'Teacher Li' has become the nickname of a famous overseas Chinese *wanghong* who runs the Twitter account @whyyoutouzhele. Its Chinese name is 'Teacher Li is not your teacher', and by the end of 2022, 'Teacher Li' had attracted 890,000 followers. Born in 1992, 'Teacher Li' was originally a 'Little Pink' who supported the rule of the CCP; however, after learning of the persecution of Chinese human rights lawyers such as Pu Zhiqiang (浦志强) through foreign websites, he gradually changed his political standpoint. Further, Li's family background may also have served as a catalyst for the change in his political viewpoint. During the Mao era, Li's grandfather was labelled a 'counter-revolutionary', and his father's experiences during the Cultural Revolution made Li realize the fate that befell a person who took a wrong political stand. When he was nineteen, Li held a personal exhibition titled 'The Circus Picasso' in the city of Ji'nan in Shandong Province, which aimed to satirize Chinese social reality. Since 2015, Li has been residing in Italy as a painter, writer and social media blogger.

From 2021, Li started to cover social problems in mainland China on Sina Blog and to accept netizens' submissions of news and publish them on his blog platform. However, because of the CCP government's control over media and news reporting, more than a dozen of Li's social media accounts were banned. As a result, Li transferred his social media reporting to Twitter and received massive attention from international followers from the commencement of the 'anti-lockdown' movement in mainland China. In November 2022, a fire in an apartment building in Urumqi of Xinjiang Province caused ten deaths. It was widely blamed on the pandemic lockdown policy as the apartment buildings were sealed off under the directives of these policies. The Urumqi fire disaster swiftly ignited the anger of Chinese people who had suffered under the 'zero-Covid' policy implemented by the CCP government, including the loss of many jobs. Consequently, on the Middle Urumqi Road of Shanghai, those furious Chinese people gathered and protested against the government's zero-Covid policy and called for the CCP and Xi Jinping to step down from power.

Prior to the Urumqi fire disaster, in October 2022, a protester hung some anti-government slogans on the Sitong Bridge (四通桥) in Beijing. These slogans labelled Xi Jinping a 'dictator' and called for him to be deposed. Instead, a Chinese president should be elected via general suffrage, and the 'zero Covid' policy ended. This brave protester was Peng Zaizhou (彭载舟). He was arrested by policemen soon after the Sitong Bridge protest, but not before he was compared with the 'Tank Man' of the 4th June Tiananmen demonstration by many Chinese political dissidents, and labelled by some media as 'Bridge Man'.[3] The Chinese government banned the reporting of this protest on China's WeChat, and blog outlets and words and phrases about the protest soon became sensitive on China's internet. The Sitong Bridge protest is considered one of those rare protest movements in Beijing since the 4th June demonstration and ushered in the 'White Paper Revolution' that happened one month later. Together, they heralded the end of the pandemic lockdown and the zero-Covid policy in mainland China.

Like the 4th June demonstration, the 'White Paper Revolution' was organized and executed mainly by China's young college students, particularly in Beijing and Shanghai. In both the Urumqi Middle Road of Shanghai and the Liangma Bridge of Beijing, young college students held up sheets of white paper, signifying that their voice has been suppressed and there was no freedom of speech and media in mainland China. Further, the white paper also represented Chinese people's eagerness to end the zero-Covid policy as the government was not listening to the people's wishes and their demands had been silenced and ignored. More than thirty years since the brutal crackdown on the 4th June demonstration, the zero-Covid policy revealed to the Chinese public the true goal of the CCP, which is not to serve the people but to maintain and consolidate its power. After more than forty years of economic growth, the Chinese people felt and realized afresh that their fate was in the hands of the CCP. This was like the situation during the Great Leap Forward and the Great Famine of the Mao era, when the CCP government and its leaders did not listen to or care about their people's voice and suffering and minded only the stability of their rule and their image on the international stage. Further, the truth of the zero-Covid policy awakened the younger generations of the Chinese, who had been immersed in material enjoyment and consumption. They were intentionally led to avoid the ideas that Chinese people deserve many rights that have been violated by the CCP, and that they need to stand up and fight for them.

During the 'White Paper Revolution', Li tweeted on 17 December 2022:

Some mainland Chinese thought the ending of the Zero-Covid policy was due to the 'White Paper Revolution' and the actions of those college students, but the fact was during that week:

The workers of Fushikang were engaged in intensive conflict

The people of Urumqi rushed the local government organisations

On the evening of the 27 November, the residents of Wuhan demonstrated on Hanzheng Street, damaging public infrastructure

And what they had in common was that they did not hold up white paper and shout out for the government to step down, but simply requested the removal of the Zero-COVID policy.

(李老师不是你老师推特, 2022)

This Twitter post of Li pointed out that it was not the 'White Paper Revolution' and those college students who participated in the movement that forced the Chinese government to end its zero-Covid policy; rather, it was the bottom-up protests from Chinese people that prompted the government decision.

In another Twitter post published on 21 December 2022, soon after the end of the zero-Covid policy, Li wrote:

I want to reiterate: in September, I anticipated the outcome of the sudden and irresponsible ending of the Zero-COVID policy, Even I knew what was going to happen, so why didn't Zhongnanhai (中南海)?[4]

What have they done for the recovery from the pandemic? What did they do when Shanghai was invaded by the highly contagious Omicron virus? What caused this irresponsible sudden ending of the zero-Covid policy? What I can say is that the government really have some experts. (李老师不是你老师推特, 2022)

In this Twitter post, Li gave voice to the complaints of millions of Chinese citizens who felt and experienced the catastrophic outcome of the CCP government's sudden and irresponsible ending of the Zero-Covid policy. Many had failed to buy any antipyretics and lost their elderly relatives because of lack of medication and medical resources in hospitals. At the end of the post, Li mocked the incapacity of the CCP government and blamed it for the people's hardships and loss of life.

Li achieved celebrity status on China's internet during the anti-zero-Covid protests because his Twitter account became the main conduit for gathering live information about the protests and demonstrations. Li tweeted videos of the demonstrations, including those titled 'There are peoples who were arrested and the public shouted out "release them"', 'Police cleared the place', 'At Middle Urumqi Road in Shanghai, people shouted out "go off duty, police"'. These were undoubtedly very sensitive in the political and social atmosphere of mainland China (直击/警人墙镇压! '防疫过当' 新疆大火10死, 上海民众聚乌鲁木齐路高喊习下台 '两车人被捕', 2022).

Many Twitter users sent Li information and reports anonymously and Li's Twitter account received around 600,000 followers within one week of the 'White Paper Revolution' breaking out. Those videos that were published on Li's Twitter account attracted more attention to the 'White Paper Revolution' from mainland Chinese netizens, and some Chinese people and reporters joined the demonstration and protest after watching the videos on Li's Twitter account. Accordingly, Li's Twitter reporting soon attracted attention from international media practitioners and became their source of firsthand information about the protests in mainland China. In an interview with *Deutsche Welle*, Li said:

> The truly great people are those who have the guts to stand out and take to the street. All I have done is to record those people's actions, and let those outside of China know what has really happened in China. If you say I am great, I do not think so. I am just a recorder, and was accidentally caught up in history.
> (《德國之聲》專訪「李老師不是你老師」：真正偉大的是敢站在街上的這些人，我只是被歷史選中的記錄者, 2022)

Because Li spread those sensitive videos and reports on his Twitter account, his family members in mainland China came under pressure from the CCP government. Moreover, Li himself expressed that he had received death threats and suffered a lot physically and mentally. On 4 December 2022, Li tweeted that there was no way he would take his own life, and he gave his picture to a CNN reporter and asked the reporter to publish it if anything happened to him. During the height of the 'White Paper Revolution', on 27 November 2022, Li published an open letter entitled 'To all the public officials who are looking for me or about to look for me' on his Twitter account in which he stated:

This Twitter account is for my own personal use; I have not and will not join any organisation.

As for why my Twitter account has gathered so many opinions, the reason is really simple: in the past more year or so, netizens have formed the habit of contributing to my Twitter account.

In other words, if the mainland Chinese media could report on what was being discussed by Chinese people, they need not to come to my Twitter account to express their innermost thoughts and feelings.

Regarding the current situation, though my Twitter account is only a personal account, I have reporters at all the emergencies and accidents happening across China.

For me, I am a painter and a person who writes crappy love stories. All of this was originally far from my life; however, your control of free speech created me.

At this moment, the suffering that resulted from my self-censorship due to fear of you has disappeared.

I am never afraid of you anymore.

I always say that I am a person who is pushed by others, which is just like what is happening to me today.

This is not my decision, as it all happened too suddenly.

Several days ago no one would have thought a fire would ignite the whole nation.

Several months ago no one would have thought that slogans from Peng Zaizhou would be called across the nation.

I know you fundamentally do not understand why a piece of white paper triggered the actions of students of dozens of universities across China.

Just like you do not understand that it is only ten human lives, only a three-year-old kid, only a traffic accident[5].

How come they have caused such a big stir?

So eventually you will blame others, and admit not even a little bit of mistake.

So, you will keep sparking the public's fury through various 'trivial matters', and your biggest mistake is that you never admit your mistakes.

Yes, I received some death threats today. I don't care whether they truly came from some of you.

In the event of my possible disappearance, I have made proper arrangements for my Twitter account and my life.

If any accident befalls me, people will take over my account immediately and journalists from major media outlets will announce the news.

As I always said, you can send me private messages, but you never make direct contact.

You only interrogate those netizens in mainland China whom you suspect and ask them if they know me; but actually, you can find me and talk to me directly.

Also, many thanks to those who are paying attention to what is happening in China.

I have been recording what is happening in China with an eye to objectivity, accuracy and timeliness.

. . .

You do not intend to make me shut up.

Because I promise, this will bring more trouble to you.

The public has become accustomed to publicising and spreading what is happening.

I am neither the first nor the last to do this.

You also do not intend to disturb my family members.

Because from the time I first challenged your censorship, I have realised the possibility of not seeing my family for the rest of my life.

The instant my family members are harmed, I will fight you.
(李老师不是你老师: 致所有正在找我和准备找我的公职人员, 2022)

In Li's open letter to public officials in mainland China, the power of social media to change the situation in China is foregrounded. Such has been forecasted and expected by many political and cultural experts and scholars.

We have reason to believe that in the foreseeable future, more and more social media personalities will spread sensitive information on the internet and that will encourage more Chinese people to stand up and fight for their rights. People like Li and Peng should be remembered by all Chinese for triggering the discussion of human rights and the government's duty and legitimacy at this very important historical juncture when Xi Jinping has consolidated his power and faced no opposition in speeding up his authoritarian rule. During the past three years when Xi implemented his unscrupulous zero-Covid policy, the fate of China and its people has landed in another unpredictable and unfortunate plight; therefore, it seems that no force can save China unless its own people stand up and fight for freedom and justice for themselves.

Li's open letter received many comments from netizens inside and outside of mainland China. Netizen 'USABelAir2021' commented: 'Come on Li Laoshi, I do not have any immediate family in mainland China, so if there is a need I can take over the account from you'; netizen 'dwell_neverland' wrote: 'They turned many common and mild people into avengers and then asked "why did you do that, who instigated you to do that?" However it was the CCP itself who incited these numerous Chinese people to resist tyranny.' Another netizen, 'Cook42756302', commented: 'If they dare to persecute Li Laoshi, there will be thousands upon thousands of Li Laoshis who arise.' Netizen 'Nick_wong2046' wrote: 'I support this. The fire of democracy will not be put out easily; instead, it will be passed down from generation to generation in the hearts of people who resist totalitarian rule.' Netizen 'Dongcanada1' wrote: 'Li Laoshi, you are a hero, and we will forever be by your side, let's fight together as the ever lonely but brave us, united now'; netizen 'wurenhua' implored: 'Pay attention to the safety of Li Laoshi! Pay tribute to Li Laoshi who spreads truth!'; and netizen 'vP9fWtLgK3DKYzr' commented: 'Bring on love and courage, and on the road to freedom and democracy, every step is worth remembering. Braveness is contagious, come on! Every person who does not want to kneel!' (李老师不是你老师：致所有正在找我和准备找我的公职人员, 2022). From these netizens' comments and messages, we can see how impacting and powerful Li Laoshi's open letter was and how much respect he enjoys in the hearts of the Chinese people; people who long for freedom, democracy, human rights and rights as a citizen to be enjoyed by every Chinese person. Most importantly, these comments attest that the courage to resist the authoritarian rule and the hope to live a freer and better life are in the hearts of many Chinese people.

Also, from Li's actions, it is easy to feel the threat and danger he faces as a *wanghong* who acts as a public activist even though he is based overseas. Because of him, one could see how brave and sincere those young college students were when they held up white paper and stood on China's streets. Many were arrested and are currently undergoing interrogation and detention. For this reason, some people published their names and identities on the internet and called for others to keep an eye on them. They claimed that they did not break any law or commit any crime in mainland China, so their safety and freedom should be secure. Only if their situations become a matter of social concern could their security and freedom be maintained.

Some people questioned Li about the large volume of his Twitter posts and the rapid growth of followers on his Twitter account. They believed that Li must have a team to help him run his Twitter account; others praised him for creating a very useful platform to expose what is truly happening in mainland China. After all, his Twitter account and posts enjoy more popularity and have more impact even when compared with large media outlets across the world. Given that Li is currently based overseas, this provided a pretext for the CCP government and 'Little Pinks' to blame 'foreign hostile forces' for interfering in domestic Chinese matters that aim to overthrow the rule of the CCP and bring chaos and disaster to China. However, in a video circulating on YouTube, when those brave young people gathered at the Liangma Bridge in Beijing to protest the zero-Covid policy and the lack of speech and media freedom in mainland China, they yelled to the camera and made it clear: 'We only represent ourselves and there are no foreign hostile forces behind us manipulating us. What do you mean by foreign forces? Do you mean Marx?'

From their mocking manner and words, it is clear that these young people do not want to be utilized and hijacked by the CCP government to attack foreign powers. They also do not believe in the Marxist Communism that has been reinforced in many Chinese universities now that Xi Jinping is the prime mover. In other words, this open mockery of Marx and Communism reveals the minds of Chinese people under CCP's authoritarian rule – a rule which is obscurantist, threatens and intimidates its people, suppresses media freedom and public activism, and purges political dissidents and rights-defence lawyers.

The significance of the 'White Paper Revolution' is that more than thirty years after the crackdown on the 4th June demonstration, the world has once again heard the voice of the educated youths of China. Hopefully, this little spark will survive and can ignite more similar movements. Because only if this happens does China have hope.

Conclusion

Throughout the discussion of this book, contemporary Chinese celebrities have been shown to be an emerging and influential force in configuring and refreshing cultural norms and moral institutions, triggering critical thinking and debate about civil and human rights, and stimulating participation in economic and political changes and progressions. Whether film or television actors, famous reporters or writers, star professors and intellectuals or internet influencers, these celebrity figures have been actively expressing their opinions and attitudes towards topical sociopolitical issues and controversial cultural and civil issues of present-day China.

Concentrating on the interaction and confrontation between celebrity and official cultures, the book has revealed and clarified the complicated bonds between mainstream culture and celebrity culture in China today. By exposing and analysing celebrity figures' activism and their challenge to the rule and legitimacy of the CCP government, the book uncovers the effects celebrity figures and stars have and their power in contesting the obscurantist rule of the CCP regime, which tries to control and manipulate the thought and opinions of its people. In present-day China – where media freedoms and the expression of ideas encounter iron-fisted surveillance and control, and where public intellectuals and opinion leaders are silenced and jailed by the government – celebrity voices seem particularly important in awakening the public's critical thinking ability, through which they challenge the rule of the Chinese government.

By studying the governance of moral transgressions, rights defence and other campaigns and movements of public concern that have been initiated and employed by contemporary Chinese celebrities and stars, the book has examined a diverse group of Chinese celebrities. These have included scandalous celebrities, celebrity public intellectuals, sports celebrities, feminist celebrities and internet celebrities, each representing different activist opinions and contesting in different areas of public and civic concern. By investigating archetypal cases of these celebrity activists, the focus of the book has revolved around how contemporary Chinese celebrities and star figures act to capture the public's attention to rethink the established moral bindings and institutions of socialist China, the obscurantist rule enforced on them by the CCP and the government's exploitation of their human, civil and political rights. Through its chapters, the book has realized its goal of foregrounding the activism of contemporary Chinese celebrities and the challenge they pose to the CCP government and its rule in mainland China, and also the influence and example that they are for the Chinese people.

The findings of Chapter 2 highlight the tenacity of the moral obligations and establishment of socialist China and how the CCP government uses moral coercion to deploy and regulate the Chinese celebrities and masses alike. Scandalous celebrities serve as a mirror, reflecting social, moral and economic stigmas that have emerged since the Opening Up period and as a consequence of the CCP's policy and governance in the economic, sociocultural and ethical domains. In the past decade, scandalous celebrities and stars have become a prism through which contemporary China's social ills, economic polemics and moral waning have been revealed. Thus, scandalous celebrities have been employed by the CCP for their utility in promoting the party's requirements. Using celebrities as negative examples, the party amends and renews its commercial, ethical and sociocultural edicts and guidelines through its governance of celebrities. In this way, celebrity figures have been proven to be a weathervane for the changeable tendencies of the party's guides and principles as it seeks to strengthen its rule and legitimacy. From another perspective, the moral transgressions and weaknesses revealed in the celebrity figures' cases expose the shaky and collapsing state of the CCP's moral rule over its citizens. Thus, in order to continue its rule and legitimacy, the current CCP government has reinstated the tightest moral regulations in entertainment and cultural circles. The famous overseas Chinese writer Yan Geling revealed in a recent interview that even drug abuse has become a taboo topic in literary creations, which illustrates how the CCP views moral control and institutions as the base of its rule over the Chinese people (严歌苓：巨大幻灭 十年一觉中国梦 担心自废武功... 2023).

In addition to the moral contestation and transgressions represented and unleashed by celebrity figures in the face of the CCP's rule, this book has studied the emerging fashions of celebrity activism in China. In the political and social scene of today's China, nearly all kinds of activism – including women's rights, human and civil rights and political rights – are restricted. One example of this was the famous 'Blank Paper' movement of late 2022, in which young college students of major cities such as Shanghai and Beijing protested the lengthy lockdown during the Covid pandemic and the lack of speech and media freedoms. Some of those young participants of the 'Blank Paper' movement were arrested and detained by the government, and so netizens of China called for attention to their plight. In the most recent case, Chinese rights-defending lawyers Ding Jiaxi (丁家喜) and Xu Zhiyong (许志永) were sentenced to twelve years in prison for the crime of 'inciting subversion of state power' (颠覆国家政权罪).

In this climate, the appearance and development of a celebrity activism in today's China that intends to bring about political and social change are of considerable importance to the Chinese people and the Chinese nation. There is scholarly consensus that celebrity activism acts as a part of the democratization of public recognition through ideological and political dedication shared by people around the world (Nayar 2021). Research also suggests that celebrity exists through forms of signification and acts as both overarching and specific discursive power; it carries politicized values and meanings, concerns and inequalities and dreams of the contemporary age (Redmond 2018). Rather than suggesting that celebrity acts as an intimidating imposition that affects society according to crushing ideologies that back the powerful elite over the general public (Meyers 2009), I have argued throughout this book that contemporary Chinese celebrities challenge the dominant and repressive ideologies and social mores by voicing their concerns about the Chinese general public and the Chinese nation. Such celebrities include famous writers, influential hosts and reporters, popular movie and TV stars and directors, star sportspeople and professors. These figures act as active embodiments of and advocates for moral reconfiguration, economic transformation, social liberation, the rights of women and political changes. In so doing, they manifest the developing trajectory of celebrity activism in China today.

Chapter 3 highlighted the efforts and contributions of contemporary Chinese celebrity intellectuals including writers, journalists and university professors in raising the public's awareness and participation in civil and human rights campaigns that challenge the rule of the CCP over mainland China. Public intellectuals and opinion leaders are a rare phenomenon in current China because they are usually either silenced or penalized by the government or enlisted by the CCP to help with their propaganda goals. The latter are selected and endorsed by the party and become pseudo public intellectuals who serve and support the rule of the CCP. In this context, courageous celebrity intellectuals such as Chai Jing (柴静), Cui Yongyuan (崔永元), Fang Fang (方方) and Yan Geling (严歌苓) have stepped forward bravely as human and civil rights activists. This deserves respect and admiration. These people risk their fame and fortune when they speak up for the everyday people and the underprivileged because they could be criticized and punished, and their performances, works and shows could be banned by the Chinese government. Yan Geling met with such a fate after she openly and boldly criticized the CCP regarding its ignorance of women's rights, its violations of human rights and its suppression of freedom of media and speech. Further, Yan mentioned in an interview that during the 1980s, Chinese literary and cultural workers enjoyed much more freedom than present; in particular, she mentioned the 4th June crackdown in Tiananmen Square, which served as a watershed between a comparatively free creative atmosphere and tight controls over the cultural and social domains (严歌苓：巨大幻灭 十年一觉中国梦 担心自废武功... 2023).

In the history of socialist China, intellectuals have incurred the cruelest suppression and persecution from the Chinese government during various social and political movements and chaos. Thus, it is widely considered that socialist China has never had great intellectuals in a real sense when compared with ancient or Republican China; rather, intellectuals and scholars have bowed to the ruling regime either by choice or by force in order to survive or prosper under communist rule. However, a society without intellectuals who speak truth to the rulers and speak up for the wider population is not a healthy one and actually a dangerous one. Unfortunately, in present-day China, the lack of voice and public opinion coming from intellectuals suits the obscurantist rule of the CCP regime, which manipulates the thought and opinion of its people and exploits their rights to critical thinking and free expression. Under these circumstances, celebrity intellectuals using their popularity and influence among the public to have their voice and opinion heard by everyday people is of great significance. This is particularly the case because the Chinese public is bombarded and overwhelmed by patriotic and nationalist propaganda, and guided and directed by socio-economic development plans that emphasize consumption. In tandem, these factors impair their critical thinking ability and desire to participate in political and civil issues and transformations.

The CCP's totalitarian efforts may be regarded as successful to some degree as there are many Little Pinks (小粉红) and citizens who support the propaganda, policies and rule of the CCP in mainland China. These policies include resisting containment by America, uniting Taiwan using military force and the suitability of one-party rule for China. If the CCP gains support for these policies from the Chinese people, who lack information from outside of China and critical thinking ability, it could be very dangerous for the entire world, leading to a global conflict sparked by the CCP regime. Therefore, different and critical voices and opinions from public and responsible intellectuals must be heard by the Chinese public. Then, they will be able to form rational opinions and decide whether they should support their government unconditionally.

Chapter 4 foregrounds the challenge coming from sporting circles to the stability of the CCP's rule. As a most disciplined cohort that receives strict coaching in patriotism and loyalty, the forces for contestation represented by famous figures in sports circles are of importance in raising the public's concern about the legitimacy of the CCP's rule. Since the height of socialism in China, famous sports figures have been honoured as national heroes and enlisted by the CCP to promote its patriotic and collective propaganda and mobilize the Chinese masses to follow and support the government's policies and rule. Sporting champions and stars have been used by the CCP as representing Chinese people's courage and persistence when China was facing blockades by countries that harboured different ideological beliefs. Thus, sports appear to have an innate connection with Chinese politics in terms of their nationalist appeal and uniting power.

However, in the recent decade, the most loyal celebrity cohorts in the sports circle of contemporary China have become a breeding ground that has not only exposed the corrupt culture in the sporting world but also brought the legitimacy of the CCP government into question. Some courageous and upstanding sports stars such as Hao Haidong (郝海东) and his wife Ye Zhaoying (叶钊颖) believe the bedlam in the micro world of sports echoes the fraud and mayhem in the macro social and official realms. Such expression of concern from sporting celebrities demonstrates novel ways that sporting stars can contribute to the construction of an ideal social and political reality in present-day China. Though the case studies examined in this chapter are rare, their significance and existence as a historic milestone ought not to be neglected. Sports stars' open defiance of the Chinese political system is unprecedented. Like the 'Bridgeman' and the 'Tankman' and those young Chinese people who participated in the 'Blank Paper' movement, these sports stars' names should be remembered by every Chinese citizen who harbours desire for freedom, equality and human rights.

Chapter 5 identified another challenge posed to the Chinese government – one that is camouflaged by the propaganda of the CCP that Chinese women enjoy equal rights with men and their rights have been secured and promoted by the CCP government. Through focusing on celebrity feminist rights defenders and activists, this chapter displayed Chinese women's improved awareness of their rights. Rather than sticking to those traditional and socialist ethical mores enforced upon them by official admonitions and propaganda, contemporary Chinese females regained their freedom in giving birth (or not) to children and by participating in the Chinese version of the #MeToo movement. In doing so, Chinese women showed their courage and power in speaking up for themselves and defending their own rights. Further, as represented by female celebrities and stars, female rights activists in China have launched their own sexual liberation campaign, which potentially will shake the moral stability and rule forced on Chinese people by the socialist state. Instead of being consumed by men, Chinese women have started to consume men in this fashion of sexual liberation that has completely overthrown the suppressive perception of sexual bonds that prevailed in socialist culture. Also, rather than being a disadvantaged gender and social group that has been rescued by the salvific figure of the CCP, these contemporary Chinese feminist rights defenders have turned themselves into an activist force. Their potential poses a threat to the idea that the rule of the Chinese government is morally binding and so the CCP has employed constraints to maintain and consolidate its rule over the Chinese people.

Chapter 6 featured some typical Chinese internet influencers who act as public rights defenders and activists. With the advancement of social media and self-media techniques and platforms, Chinese *wanghong* have become an enormous social and civil force in present-day mainland China through involving themselves in defending human and civil rights and protesting against the authoritarian rule of the CCP. In particular, this chapter investigated Chinese internet celebrities' participation, effect and influence in Covid-19 news reporting and the most recent protests against Covid-19 lockdowns. Case studies of *wanghong* independent reporter Chen Qiushi (陈秋实) and 'Li Laoshi is not your teacher' revealed that Chinese internet celebrities have played an independent and critical role in building a public sphere and promoting citizens' rights and political change. In their coverage of the 'Blank Paper' movement, those *wanghong* reporters became the most reliable sources of information on the progression of the movement, indicating their influence among the Chinese public and their power in challenging the surveillance and monitoring conducted by the CCP government on media outlets and expression.

From various perspectives, the book's chapters have studied diverse celebrity figures and cohorts and the challenge they pose for the control and manipulation of the CCP government on mainland Chinese citizens. Further, the book's chapters have exposed celebrity figures' power to promote the media freedoms and civil and human rights of Chinese citizens, and to question the political system and legitimacy of rule of the CCP regime. In summary, Chapter 2 demonstrated how the CCP has introduced and effected adjustments in the moral, economic, social and cultural arenas through celebrity governance. Chapters 3 to 6 uncovered celebrity activism in different spheres of contemporary China, and thus provided a comprehensive and vital portrayal and reading of celebrity activism in China today. The value of this book is that through its practical focus on the Chinese celebrity scene, it has mapped out contemporary Chinese celebrity governance and activism.

Notes

Chapter 1

1 'Tying a white wolf with bare hands' is a popular Chinese saying that is used to describe immoral practices in financial markets. In present-day China, some rich business people and celebrities (riding on their popularity and close connections with influential business people) use a small amount of money to leverage big commercial or financial projects, which easily attract blind investments from small stakeholders; however, those rich people cash out their benefits once the projects have absorbed a large amount of public investment, thereby leaving the small stakeholders trapped in those failing projects.

2 The famous Chinese writer Yan Geling's (严歌苓) novel *Xiuxiu: The Sent Down Girl* (天浴) was adapted into a film of the same title by Chinese actress Chen Chong (陈冲) in 1998. It tells the story of a sent-down girl who has to bribe the local village government cadre with sex in order to return to her home city. The suffering of the girl and her miserable death reveals the trauma of millions of China's sent-down youths during the Cultural Revolution era, which led to the film's banning in mainland China.

3 Soon after becoming the new General Secretary of the CCP in 2012, Xi Jinping, with the help of Wang Qishan (王岐山), removed the following officials: Xu Caihou and Guo Boxiong (the former Vice-Chairmen of the Central Military Commission, which is the country's top military council); Zhou Yongkang (a retired senior leader of the CCP, former member of the 17th Politburo Standing Committee and former Secretary of the Central Political and Legislative Affairs Committee); and Ling Jihua (one of the principal political advisers to Hu Jintao, and the former Director of the General Office of the CCP Central Committee). These high-grade corrupt officials and ex-officials were the so-called "big tigers" and the new Gang of Four (the most powerful of the corrupt officials) in Chinese politics, and their defeat by Xi and his colleagues was applauded by most Chinese people. The competence, fortitude and valour of the Xi Jinping administration

in its quest to eliminate official corruption has attracted great attention from the rest of the world and offered hope and reassurance to the Chinese people that their government institutions may now become less corrupt and fairer and more capable. Some political pundits believe that Xi Jinping's iron-fisted crackdown on the new Gang of Four did not arise from his goal of eradicating corruption from within government, but was instead a wish to expel and purge political adversaries from other factions of the CCP, and to reshuffle and consolidate his own power base. Likewise, it is the strong view of many political commentators that Bo Xilai's conspiracy with Zhou Yongkang and Xu Caihou to threaten the power of Xi Jinping served as the underlying reason for Xi's expulsion of him and his accomplices (Wang 2014: 235; Tiezzi 2015).

4   In early 2022, a Chinese netizen published a self-media report that told the story of a middle-aged Chinese village woman with schizophrenia who had been abducted and sold to a man in a village in Xuzhou, Jiangsu Province. The woman was assumed to have been tortured by the man and his relatives, forced to marry him, and to give birth to eight children now aged between three and their early twenties. In the news report published alongside the self-media article, a photo showed a woman with chains on her neck staying in a very dilapidated room without enough food and clothes to sustain her through the harsh winter. The woman also showed signs of mental disorder. This report triggered hot debate and criticism among Chinese netizens and the public regarding women's rights in contemporary China, the corruption of local government officials and human rights concerns. Both freelance journalists and the local government in Xuzhou conducted investigations into the woman's case; however, the Chinese public could not agree with the government's conclusion that the woman had been formally married to the man who chained her and she might have had mental health problems before she married the man. The government's attitudes and its dereliction of duty sparked anger among Chinese people and forced them to consider the reality of human rights in contemporary China.

5   At the outset of the Opening Up reforms, and without their work units' (单位) permission, many singers and actors went to villages and towns to perform at parties to earn extra money above their fixed salary from their work units. Further, Liu Xiaoqing's engagement with the new trend of being self-employed mirrored the aspirations of many people who longed and endeavoured to rid themselves of the constraints of the state-run work units. These people wanted to try their luck in the free and profitable business world enabled by the newly implemented privatised market economy at the height of the reform era. Liu Xiaoqing's ambitions grew while she made more money, and she did

not quit moonlighting until she decided to formally engage in business by establishing her own company—Beijing Xiaoqing Culture and Arts Co. Ltd (北京晓庆文化艺术有限责任公司) in 1995. At the peak of her business career, Liu Xiaoqing served as the representative of up to 26 companies affiliated with her own company in different ways, and her businesses ranged from beverages, handbags, clothing and cosmetics to construction and real estate. The overall investments of these companies surpassed 5 billion *yuan*. In 1999, Liu Xiaoqing was ranked number 45 in Forbes magazine's list of China's 50 richest individuals ('China's 50 Richest Businessmen' 1999).

Chapter 2

1   From another perspective, scandals could attract more attention to a celebrity especially under the current 'eyeball' economy system. For Liu Xiaoqing, her life in jail created enormous curiosity from her fans and foes. Even the cheap cosmetics she used in prison became dinner-party material, which showed how influential celebrities and stars were in the Chinese social and cultural scenes. Depending on her maverick personality and progressive thinking, Liu Xiaoqing successfully fashioned herself into a cultural icon of contemporary China.

2   For example, the young mainland actor Liu Ye played a foot soldier of the Liberation Army when it was entering Beijing, and he has only one line in the whole film: 'Report! I am a veteran of the 28th Regiment of the Red Army. I salute Central Committee Member Mao on behalf of veteran Red Army soldiers, dead or alive!' The Chinese audience has been fed up with such revolutionary clichés; but in *The Founding*, when it is articulated by Liu Ye, a promising young actor with attractive looks and good acting skills, such words acquire charm and even star power through his powerful voice, however hoarse.

3   Ge You is employed to play a Red Army soldier who takes part in the battle to 'liberate' Beijing. When the soldiers arrive at the old city wall of Beijing, Ge You demonstrates his unique wit and remarks: 'In front there is a courtyard of a landlord, which is extremely solid, and we cannot bomb it by grenade. Therefore we request artillery aid.' Here, by juxtaposing Beijing city with the courtyard of a landlord, the simple logic of a peasant soldier is demonstrated and an ideological implication is woven between the lines. Fan Wei, another very influential *xiaopin* (小品, witty skit) comedian also joined the performance. As the regular partner of Zhao Benshan in his *xiaopin* works, Fan Wei is one of most popular faces on the stage of the annual CCTV Spring Festival Gala. In *The Founding*, Fan Wei plays

Mao Zedong's cook, an honest and sincere peasant figure who is extremely loyal to Mao. When Mao gives him a cigarette, he is reluctant to smoke it but stores it over his ear. As he has played the role of a stupid young man in Zhao Benshan's *xiaopin* series *Selling Crunches and Selling Wheel Chair* many times, the foolish image of Fan Wei has taken root in the mind of the common viewers, which coincidentally reinforces the honest, sincere and loyal characteristics of the cook in *The Founding* (Li 2010: 63).

4   The similarities between the historical figures and the celebrities in regard to appearance and temperament are obvious in *The Founding*. For example, from the outer appearance of Fang Yuxiang and Chen Kaige, of Du Yuesheng and Feng Xiaogang, of Mao Renfeng and Jiangwen and of Chang Chingkuo and Chen Kun, the resemblances are easily detected. Some viewers are attracted by the star-version of the historical figures and therefore become interested in historical facts, such that the historical figures played by celebrities secure a more engaged audience for the film and bring more attention to the history (Zeng 2010: 61)—a history enforced by the Party propaganda organs on the common people. Feng Yuxiang is widely recognised as a progressive general of the Nationalist Party. In *The Founding*, he uses metaphor to hint at corrupt politics under the rule of the Nationalist Party. Chen Kaige is employed to play the Feng Yuxiang role not only because of their similar appearance but also because of the cultural and celebratory privileges Chen Kaige enjoys among viewers. Chen Kaige is an internationally awarded director and he still has much impact on the domestic and international film markets. The themes of Chen's films always revolve around grand narratives and solemn topics, as Gong and Yang describe them: 'sublime allegorical cinema of the grand narrative' (2010: 15), making him a serious director with historical consciousness and integrity, which is coincidentally similar to the temperament of the Feng Yuxiang figure.

Chapter 4

1   In 2012, CCP cadres Lei Zhengfu, who was the Party leader of Beipei District of the city of Chongqing, and Sun Dejiang, the former representative of the National People's Congress of Shuangcheng City of Heilongjiang Province, were exposed by their mistresses through Weibo. Lei's sex tapes and photos with his lover were posted and news of Sun's sexual harassment of a local television presenter was released. Normally, the disclosure of their moral misconduct with their mistresses is just the tip of the iceberg of the entire criminal deportment of corrupt officials,

which generally includes the acceptance of bribes, embezzlement of public funds and other acts in violation of the law. Therefore, the media exposure of the 'third party' of many Chinese corrupt officials has often led to discovery of their other corrupt behaviours. Under common circumstances, once their moral and sex-related corrupt behaviours are exposed, the 'evil' officials' careers in Chinese officialdom are ended.

Chapter 5

1 According to Xu and his colleagues' research findings, 'the traditional mindset of males being superior and females inferior still exists in some economically undeveloped areas and constrains many women. With their lower education level and economic independence, many victims have no idea of their legal rights and the methods to protect their rights. This is common in rural households with a higher incidence of domestic violence. As a result, victims do not seek legal help in the first place but choose informal help, including extended family members, friends and community members, to deal with violence. However, as survivors' relationships decline, they are more likely to seek support from a broader range of sources. In China, the police usually identify IPV events, including most domestic violence cases, as ordinary family disputes without, or with little, criminal justice intervention. Mediation, especially oral mediation by police officers, is still the most-used method of handling of these kinds of events. Therefore, cultural customs and traditional values affect the accurate analysis of IPV prevalence in China' (Xu et al. 2022: 3).

2 Hong Huang has multiple identities: she is a woman from an illustrious family; a female entrepreneur; an amateur actor; and a prose writer of female love and sex. With the publication of her autobiographical book, *My Abnormal Life* (*Wo de feizhengchang shenghuo*, 2007), Hong reveals her work and family life to the curious reading public, who have been keen to look into her famous life. Hong is the granddaughter of Zhang Shizhao (1881–1973), a famous educator and politician of the Republic era (1912–1949); daughter of Zhang Hanzhi (1935–2008) (Zhang Shizhao's daughter), Chairman Mao Zedong's (1893–1976) English teacher and the wife of a previous Minister of Foreign Affairs (Qiao Guanhua [1913–1983]); and the wife of Chen Kaige (b. 1952), the internationally celebrated Chinese Fifth generation director. With her bold appeal to contemporary Chinese women to act liberally regarding their love and sexual issues, Hong Huang deserves to be called a genuine 'high-born ruffian feminist'.

3 Muzi Mei was born in 1978 and graduated from a university in Guangzhou. After her graduation, she worked as a journalist for a newspaper. The *Rock and Roll Pop Star Event*, which is a well-known blog entry of Muzi's, also published in *Diary of Sexual Love,* made Muzi famous (or infamous) overnight. This diary entry recounts her sexual experiences with a pop star, and the detailed depiction of her experiences is extremely bold and brazen.

4 Although *Diary of Sexual Love* was banned immediately after it was released, its legal version still sold more than 100,000 copies.

Chapter 6

1 According to Kieran Press-Reynolds, 'Austin Li Jiaqi, who is known as the 'Lipstick King' and has over 64 million followers on live-stream platform Taobao Live, was streaming on Friday night when his broadcast shut off. Along with a co-host, he had brought out a plate of the British brand Viennetta's ice cream stacked with Oreos and other chocolate, all of which came together to form a tank shape, according to CNN … Jiaqi's disappearance has sparked significant discussion on Chinese social media, with Weibo hashtags relating to the situation amassing over 100 million views on Monday, according to Singapore-based news outlet The Straits Times. Some viewers and social media users have apparently found out about the massacre not through Jiaqi's ice cream formation, but by looking into why he has vanished online and seeing mentions of Tiananmen Square' (Press-Reynolds 2022).

2 Li Wenliang was a young doctor in Wuhan who circulated the information of the coronavirus in his WeChat friends circle at the very beginning of the outbreak. After doing so, Li was forced to signed a letter of admonition from the government for 'spreading false information', as at that stage of the pandemic the CCP government was still trying to cover up the truth of the virus. Later, Li himself caught the virus and unfortunately passed away in February 2019. Widely regarded as the 'whistle blower' of the pandemic, Li is remembered as a spokesperson for freedom of speech and media in China. Many Chinese people pay tribute to him, especially on the anniversaries of his death.

3 During the crackdown on the 4th June demonstration in 1989, the CCP government used tanks to clear Tiananmen Square. A brave Chinese person stood in front of one of the tanks to block its travel. This moment was recorded by many reporters and became the most iconic moment in the 4th June demonstration. The brave person was later labelled the 'Tank Man' and enjoys great honour in the

hearts of China's pro-democracy political activists and the general public. Thus, to name Peng Zaizhou the 'Bridge Man' showed people's respect of his courage and bravery, and marked the Sitong Bridge protest as an important historical moment in contemporary China.

4 'Zhongnanhai' (中南海) was once a garden in the Imperial City, Beijing. It now serves as the central headquarters for the CCP and the State Council of China. Zhongnanhai houses the office of the CCP General Secretary and office of the Chinese Premier. The term 'Zhongnanhai' is closed linked with the central government and senior CCP officials. It is often used as a metonym for the Chinese leadership at large (Wikipedia).

5 On 24 November 2022, a fire broke out in a residential high-rise apartment building in a Uyghur-majority neighborhood in Xinjiang, China, which killed ten Uyghurs and an additional nine were injured. Journalists raised questions of whether China's strict enforcement of the zero-COVID policy prevented residents from leaving the building or interfered with the efforts of firefighters. Chinese authorities have denied these claims. The fire has been called a trigger of protests in several cities across China and in several other countries targeting the Chinese government's zero-COVID policy, but in several instances also called for an end to Chinese Communist Party (CCP)'s one-party rule and for general secretary Xi Jinping to step down (Wikipedia).

References

Cai, S. (2016), *State Propaganda in China's Entertainment Industry*, London: Routledge.

Chang, M. G. (1999), 'The Good, the Bad, and the Beautiful: Movie Actresses and Public Discourse in Shanghai, 1920s–1930s', in Y. Zhang (ed.), *Cinema and Urban Culture in Shanghai, 1922–1943*, 128–59, Stanford: Stanford University Press.

'China's 50 Richest Businessmen' (1999). Available online: https://www.forbes.com/global/1999/1115/0223059s2.html#7465a7235e39.

Dyer, R. (1998), *Stars*, London: BFI Publishing.

Gerdes, E. (2008), 'Contemporary Yangge: The Moving History of a Chinese Folk Dance Form', *Asian Theatre Journal*, 25 (1): 138–47.

Holm, D. (1991), *Art and Ideology in Revolutionary China*, Oxford: Clarendon Press.

Jeffreys, E. (2006), 'Debating the Legal Regulation of Sex-related Bribery and Corruption in the People's Republic of China', in E. Jeffreys (ed.), *Sex and Sexuality in China*, 159–78, New York: Routledge.

Jeffreys, E. and L. Edwards (2010), 'Celebrity/China', in L. P. Edwards and E. Jeffreys (eds), *Celebrity in China*, 1–20, Hong Kong: Hong Kong University Press.

Jinxing Xiu (2015), 'Interview with Liu Xiaoqing by *Jin Xing's Jin Xing Show* (*Jinxing Xiu* on 16 Dec)'. Available online: https://www.youtube.com/watch?v=9EfpM0fD7rI.

Kaikkonen, M. (1990), 'Laughable Propaganda: Modern Xiangsheng as Didactic Entertainment', PhD diss., Stockholm University Institute of Oriental Languages, Stockholm, Sweden.

Larkin, K. (2009), 'Star Power: Models for Celebrity Political Activism', *Virginia Sports and Entertainment Law Journal*, 9 (1): 155–80.

Link, P. (1984), 'The Genie and the Lamp: Revolutionary *Xiangsheng*', in B. S. McDougall (ed.), *Popular Chinese Literature and Performing Arts in the People's Republic of China 1949–1979*, 83–111, Berkeley: University of California Press.

Link, P. (2007), 'The Crocodile Bird: *Xiangsheng* in the Early 1950s', in J. Brown and P. G. Pickowicz (eds), *Dilemmas of Victory: The Early Years of the People's Republic of China*, 207–31, Cambridge, MA: Harvard University Press.

Liu, X. (1983), 我的路 (My road), Hong Kong: Yuanfang Publishing House and COMN Publication Ltd.

Liu, X. (1995), 我的自白录：从电影明星到亿万富姐 (My confessions: From film star to female billionaire), Shanghai: Shanghai Literature and Arts Press. Available online: http://books.sina.com/bg/novel/lxqconfession/index.html.

Ma, J. (1980), 相声艺术漫谈 (Informal discussion on *xiangsheng*), Guangdong: Guangdong People's Press.

Mackerras, C. (1981), *The Performing Arts in Contemporary China*, London and Boston: Routledge & Kegan Paul.

Meyers, E. (2009), 'Can You Handle My Truth: Authenticity and the Celebrity Star Image', *The Journal of Popular Culture*, 42 (5): 890–907.

Nayar, P. K. (2021), *Essays in Celebrity Culture: Stars and Styles*, London: Anthem Press.

Redmond, S. (2018), *Celebrity*, London: Taylor & Francis.

Shum, D. (2021), *Red Roulette* (红色赌盘), London: Simon & Schuster.

Siedel, J. (2021), 'China Erases Billionaire Actress Zhao Wei from History'. Available online: https://www.news.com.au/technology/online/internet/china-erases-billionaire-actress-zhao-wei-from-history/news-story/94100f6569377078cfeee411f5fc3538.

Tiezzi, S. (2015), 'Zhou Yongkang's Greatest Crime', *The Diplomat Magazine*, 21 April. Available online: http://www.wenxuecity.com/news/2015/04/28/4225327.html.

Wang, C. (2014), 周永康集团 (The Zhou Yongkang Group), Hong Kong: Hong Kong University of Finance and Economics.

Webster-Cheng, S. (2008), 'Composing, Revising and Performing Suzhou Ballads: A Study of Political Control and Artistic Freedom in Tanci, 1949–1964', PhD diss., University of Pittsburg.

Wing-Fai, L. (2014), 'Zhang Ziyi: The New Face of Chinese Femininity', in Leung Wing-Fai and Andy Wills (eds), *East Asian Film Stars*, 65–80, New York: Palgrave Macmillan.

Xiang, S. (2008), '论相声传统的继承与发展' (Commentary on the inheritance and development of the traditions of xiangsheng performance), 湖南第一师范学报, 8 (3): 155–7.

Xue, B. (1985), 中国的传统相声 (Traditional *xiangsheng* performance of China), Beijng: People's Press.

Yang Lan Fangtanlu (2012), 'Interview with Liu Xiaoqing by *Yang Lan's One on One* (*Yang Lan Fangtanlu* in 2012)'. Available online: http://v.youku.com/v_show/id_XNDY3MzUzODI4.html.

You, Z. (2012), 'Tradition and Ideology: Creating and Performing New *Gushi* in China, 1962–1966', *Asian Ethnology*, 71 (2): 259–80.

Zhang, T. (2021), 'What Does China's Crackdown on Celebrity Culture Mean for Luxury?' *Women's Wear Daily*, 20 September. Available online: https://wwd.com/fashion-news/fashion-features/china-crackdown-celebrity-culture-mean-for-luxury-1234923453/.

Chapter 2

Birtles, B. (2021), 'Kris Wu Faces Rape Charges, Triggering Debate on China's #MeToo Movement and Celebrity Culture', *ABC News*, 6 August. Available online: https://www.abc.net.au/news/2021-08-06/china-pop-star-kris-wu-accused-of-rape/100344650.

Chen, G. (1997), 我和刘晓庆：不得不说的故事 (Me and Liu Xiaoqing: The stories must be told). Available online: http://www.shuku.net/novels/xiaoqing/xiaoqing.html.

Cui, S. (2003), *Women through the Lens: Gender and Nation in a Century of Chinese Cinema*, Honolulu: University of Hawaii Press.

Donald, S. H., Y. Hong and M. Keane (2002), *Media in China: Consumption, Content and Crisis*, London: Routledge.

Dyer, R. and P. McDonald (1998), *Stars*, London: British Film Institute.

Frame, G. (2020), 'The Cultural Politics of Jennifer Lawrence as Star, Actor, Celebrity', *New Review of Film and Television Studies*, 18 (3): 345–68.

Gies, L. (2011), 'Stars Behaving Badly', *Feminist Media Studies*, 11 (3): 347–61.

Gong, H. and X. Yang (2010), 'Digitized Parody: The Politics of *Egao* in Contemporary China', *China Information*, 24 (1): 3–26.

Guo, S. (2016), 'Ruled by Attention: A Case Study of Professional Digital Attention Agents at Sina.com and the Chinese Blogosphere', *International Journal of Cultural Studies*, 19 (4): 407–23.

Hermes, J. and J. Kooijman (2016), 'The Everyday Use of Celebrities', in D. Marshall and S. Redmond (eds), *The Blackwell Companion to Celebrity*, 463–82, Malden: WileyBlackwell.

Honig, E. (2003), 'Socialist Sex: The Cultural Revolution Revisited', *Modern China*, 29 (2): 143–75.

'胡锦涛: 推动社会主义文化大发展大繁荣' (Hu Jintao: Promote the great development and prosperity of socialist culture) (2010). Available online: http://ca.china-embassy.gov.cn/chn/xwdt/201007/t20100730_4766907.htm.

Inglis, F. (2010), *A Short History of Celebrity*, Princeton: Princeton University Press.

Jeffreys, E. (2011), 'Zhang Ziyi and China's Celebrity–Philanthropy Scandals', *PORTAL Journal of Multidisciplinary International Studies*, 8 (1): pages not available.

Jeffreys, E. (2012), 'Modern China's Idols', *PORTAL Journal of Multidisciplinary International Studies*, 9 (1): pages not available.

Jeffreys, E. and L. Edwards (2010), 'Celebrity/China', in L. Edwards and E. Jeffreys (eds), *Celebrity in China*, 1–20, Hong Kong: Hong Kong University Press.

Larkin, K. G. (2009), 'Star Power: Models for Celebrity Political Activism', *Entertainment and Sports Law Journal*, 9 (1): 155–80.

Liu, X. (1995), 我的自白录：从电影明星到亿万富姐 (My confessions: From a film star to a female billionaire), Shanghai: Shanghai Literature and Arts Press. Available online: http://books.sina.com/bg/novel/lxqconfession/index.html.

Lu, J. and Y. Qiu (2013), 'Microblogging and Social Change in China', *Asian Perspective*, 37 (3): 305–31.

Lu, S. H. (2007), *Chinese Modernity and Global Biopolitics: Studies in Literature and Visual Culture*, Honolulu: University of Hawaii Press.

Marshall, D. P. and S. Redmond (2016), 'Introduction', in D. Marshall and S. Redmond (eds), *The Blackwell Companion to Celebrity*, 1–13, Malden: Wiley-Blackwell.

Nayar, P. K. (2021), *Essays in Celebrity Culture: Stars and Styles*, London and New York: Anthem Press.

Ni, C. (2002), 'Now This Is Bad Publicity', *Los Angeles Times*, 30 September. Available online: https://www.latimes.com/archives/la-xpm-2002-sep-30-fg-star30-story.html.

Penfold, R. (2004), 'The Star's Image, Victimization and Celebrity Culture', *Punishment and Society*, 6 (3): 289–302.

Peng, F. (2010), '郭德纲：从相声大师到三俗代表' (Guo Degang: From *xiangsheng* master to representative of the 'Three Vulgarities'), 记者观察: 66–8.

Pollock, T. G., Y. Mishina and Y. Seo (2016), 'Falling Stars: Celebrity, Infamy, and the Fall from (and Return to) Grace', in D. Palmer, K. Smith-Crowe and R. Greenwood (eds), *Organizational Wrongdoing: Key Perspectives and New Directions*, 235–69, Cambridge: Cambridge University Press.

'人民日报评吴亦凡被刑拘：法律面前没有顶流' (2021). Available online: https://weibo.com/2803301701/Krllk7p8u.

Ribke, N. (2015), *A Genre Approach to Celebrity Politics: Global Patterns of Passage from Media to Politics*, New York: Palgrave Macmillan.

Siedel, J. (2021), 'China Erases Billionaire Actress Zhao Wei from History'. Available online: https://www.news.com.au/technology/online/internet/china-erases-billionaire-actress-zhao-wei-from-history/news-story/94100f6569377078cfeee411f5fc3538.

Stockmann, D. and M. E. Gallagher (2011), 'Remote Control: How the Media Sustain Authoritarian Rule in China', *Comparative Political Studies*, 44 (4): 436–67.

Sullivan, J. and S. Kehoe (2018), 'Truth, Good and Beauty: The Politics of Celebrity in China', *The China Quarterly*, 237: 241–56.

Wang, H. (2009), '解读建国大业: 主流政治片的时代魅力' (Understanding *The Founding of A Republic*: The charm of mainstream political movies), 观察与思考, 19: 58.

Wang, H. and F. Shi (2018), 'Weibo Use and Political Participation: The Mechanism Explaining the Positive Effect of Weibo Use on Online Political Participation among College Students in Contemporary China', *Information, Communication & Society*, 21 (4): 516–30.

Wen, H. (2013), *Television and the Modernization Ideal in 1980s China: Dazzling the Eyes*, Lanham: Lexington Books.

'吴亦凡们不能只讲名利不知敬畏' (2021). Available online: https://news.sina.cn/gn/2021-08-19/detail-ikqcfncc3726657.d.html.

Yuan, X. (2007), '郭德纲相声的意义与缺失' (The significance and loss of the Guo Degang phenomenon'), 艺术百家, 95 (2): 163–5.

Zhang, T. (2021), 'What Does China's Crackdown on Celebrity Culture Mean for Luxury?' Available online: https://wwd.com/fashion-news/fashion-features/china-crackdown-celebrity-culture-mean-for-luxury-1234923453/.

Zhu, Y. (2008), *Television in Post-Reform China: Serial Dramas, Confucian Leadership and the Global Television Market*, London: Routledge.

Chapter 3

Braester, Y. (2010), *Painting the City Red: Chinese Cinema and the Urban Contract*, Durham: Duke University Press.

'不允许反战的国家：女艺人金星、柯蓝为乌克兰发声被禁言' (2022). Available online: https://www.rfa.org/mandarin/Xinwen/7-03022022123707.html.

Cashmore, E. (2006), *Celebrity/Culture*, London: Routledge.

'柴静演讲为什么被封杀，央视为什么封杀柴静原因揭秘' (2022). Available online: http://www.wljyyjy.com/YanJiangGao/346941.html.

'崔永元近况受瞩 参股公司及法人被限制消费' (2021). Available online: https://guojiribao.com/?p=38525.

'崔永元还活着吗央视对他的态度是可定的' (2021). Available online: https://www.zouhong365.com/zixun/yule/9738.html.

'俄媒移花接木抹黑乌军抢劫中国媒体学舌' (2022). Available online: https://www.voacantonese.com/a/Factcheck-Russia-then-China-Distort-Canadian-snipers-Ukraine-War-Tale/6598754.html.

Emilie, R. (2015), *Stars for Freedom: Hollywood, Black Celebrities, and the Civil Rights Movement*, Seattle and London: University of Washington Press.

Fan, S. (2006), '透视郭德纲相声', 投资北京, 3: 84–7.

Fletcher, R. (2015), 'Blinded by the Stars? Celebrity, Fantasy, and Desire in Neoliberal Environmental Governance', *Celebrity Studies*, 6 (4): 457–70.

Gies, L. (2009), 'Celebrity Big Brother, Human Rights and Popular Culture', *Entertainment and Sports Law Journal*, 7 (1): 2.

Guo, S. (2016), 'Ruled by Attention: A Case Study of Professional Digital Attention Agents at Sina.com and the Chinese Blogosphere', *International Journal of Cultural Studies*, 19 (4): 407–23.

Hood, J. (2010), 'Celebrity Philanthropy: The Cultivation of China's HIV/AIDS Heroes', in L. Edwards and E. Jeffreys (eds), *Celebrity in China*, 85–102. Hong Kong: Hong Kong University Press.

Hood, J. (2015), 'Peng Liyuan's Humanitarianism: Morality, Politics and Eyeing the Present and Past', *Celebrity Studies*, 6 (4): 414–29.

'环保部长: 我完整看了 "穹顶之下" 柴静没给我增加压力' (2015). Available online: https://ent.ifeng.com/a/20150302/42262401_0.shtml.

Huliaras, A. and N. Tzifakis (2010), 'Celebrity Activism in International Relations: In Search of a Framework for Analysis', *Global Society*, 24 (2): 255–74.

Jain, K., I. Sharma and A. Behl (2021), 'Voice of the Stars: Exploring the Outcomes of Online Celebrity Activism', *Journal of Strategic Marketing*, doi: 10.1080/0965254X.2021.2006275.

Jeffreys, E. (2016), 'Political Celebrities and Elite Politics in Contemporary China', *China Information*, 30 (1): 58–80.

Jeffreys, E. and L. Edwards (2010), 'Celebrity/China', in L. Edwards and E. Jeffreys (eds), *Celebrity in China*, 1–20, Hong Kong: Hong Kong University Press.

'贾樟柯: 不能把中国电影只做成主旋律的专卖场' (2022). Available online: https://ent.sina.com.cn/m/c/2022-07-08/doc-imizmscv0602703.shtml.

'经济学人: 习近平培育了一种丑陋的中国式民族主义' (2022). Available online: https://www.1688.com.au/world/china/2022/07/20/1268155.

Kapoor, I. (2012), *Celebrity Humanitarianism: The Ideology of Global Charity*, London: Routledge.

'看看支持和反对方方的专家都有谁？' (2020). Available online: https://zhuanlan.zhihu.com/p/133760882.

Kellner, D. (2010), 'Celebrity Diplomacy, Spectacle and Barack Obama', *Celebrity Studies*, 1 (1): 121–3.

Link, P. (1984), 'The Genie and the Lamp: Revolutionary *Xiangsheng*', in B. S. McDougall (ed.), *Popular Chinese Literature and Performing Arts in the People's Republic of China 1949-1979*, 83–111, London: University of California Press.

Liu, Y. (2010), '浅析郭德纲的语言特色', 文艺评论, 3: 75–6.

Lu, J. and Y. Qiu (2013), 'Microblogging and Social Change in China', *Asian Perspective* 37 (3): 305–31.

Marshall, D. (1997), *Celebrity and Power: Fame in Contemporary Culture*, Minneapolis and London: University of Minnesota Press.

Marshall, D. (2014), *Celebrity and Power: Fame in Contemporary Culture*, 2nd Edition, Kindle Edition, Minneapolis: University of Minnesota Press.

Nayar, P. K. (2021), *Essays in Celebrity Culture: Stars and Styles*, London and New York: Anthem Press.

'上海 留下一篇篇刻骨铭心的血泪文章' (2022). Available online: https://info.51.ca/articles/1088375.

Soukup, C. (2006), 'Hitching a Ride on a Star: Celebrity, Fandom, and Identification on the World Wide Web', *Southern Communication Journal*, 71 (4): 319–37.

Street, J. (2004), 'Celebrity Politicians: Popular Culture and Political Representation', *British Journal of Politics and International Relations*, 6 (4): 435–52.

Sullivan, J. and S. Kehoe (2018), 'Truth, Good and Beauty: The Politics of Celebrity in China', *The China Quarterly*, 237: 241–56.

Turner, G. (2004), *Understanding Celebrity*, London: SAGE Publications.

Wagner, K. B. (2013), 'Jia Zhangke's Neoliberal China: The Commodification and Dissipation of the Proletarian in *The World*', *Inter-Asia Cultural Studies*, 14 (3): 361–77.

Wang, H. and F. Shi (2018), 'Weibo Use and Political Participation: The Mechanism Explaining the Positive Effect of Weibo Use on Online Political Participation among College Students in Contemporary China', *Information, Communication & Society*, 21 (4): 516–30.

Wheeler, M. (2013), *Celebrity Politics: Image and Identity in Contemporary Political Communications*, Cambridge: Polity Press.

Wong, J., C. Lee, V. K. Long, D. Wu and G. M. Jones (2021), '"Let's Go, Baby Forklift!": Fandom Governance and the Political Power of Cuteness in China', *Social Media + Society*, 7: 1–18.

Xiang, S. (2008), '论相声传统的继承与发展', 河南第一师范学报, 8 (3): 155–7.

'宣布'大上海保卫战赢了'歌手写歌'老百姓信你个鬼' (2022). Available online: https://m.wenxuecity.com/news/2022/06/29/11657773.html.

Yuan, X. (2007), '郭德纲相声的意义与缺失', 艺术百家, 95 (2): 163–5.

'中国女星曾因 "反战" 遭围剿！不惧网暴再度喊话' (2022). Available online: https://www.1688.com.au/culture/entertainment/2022/04/11/1216075.

'周孝正严歌苓视频对话 '母亲啊母亲'：批评习近平就是个人贩子' (2022). Available online: https://www.youtube.com/watch?v=gKHXXBtyzlc.

Chapter 4

Andrews, D. and S. Jackson (2001), 'Introduction: Sport Celebrities, Public Culture, and Private Experience Sport Stars', in D. Andrews and S. Jackson (eds), *The Cultural Politics of Sporting Celebrity*, 1–19, London and New York: Routledge.

Archetti, E. (2001), 'The Spectacle of a Heroic Life: The Case of Diego Maradona', in D. Andrews and S. Jackson (eds), *The Cultural Politics of Sporting Celebrity*, 151–63, London and New York: Routledge.

Arendt, H. (1986), *The Origins of Totalitarianism*, London: A. Deutsch.

Bale, J. (2001), 'Nyandika Maiyoro and Kipchoge Keino: Transgression, Colonial Rhetoric and the Postcolonial Athlete', in D. Andrews and S. Jackson (eds), *The Cultural Politics of Sporting Celebrity*, 218–30, London and New York: Routledge.

Barmé, G. (1995), 'To Screw Foreigners Is Patriotic: China's Avant-Garde Nationalists', *The China Journal*, 34: 209–34.

Becker, A. (2013), 'Star Power? Advocacy, Receptivity, and Viewpoints on Celebrity Involvement in Issue Politics', *Atlantic Journal of Communication*, 21 (1): 1–16.

Dayan, D. and K. Elihu (1992), *Media Events*, Cambridge, MA: Harvard University Press.

Dikötter, F. (2010), *The History of China's Most Devastating Catastrophe 1958–1962: Mao's Great Famine*, New York: Walker Publishing Company, Inc.

'Dumped Chinese TV Host Ji Yingnan Reveals "Treacherous Official" Fan Yue's Lavish Lifestyle', *International Business Times*, posted on 18 June 2013.

Foucault, M. (1979), *Discipline and Punish: The Birth of the Prison*, trans. A. Sheridan, New York: Vintage Books.

Foucault, M. (1980), 'Prison Talk, an Interview with J.-J. Brochier', in C. Gordon (ed.), *Power/Knowledge: Selected Interviews and Other Writings 1972–1977*, trans. C. Gordon, L. Marshall, J. Mepham and K. Soper, 37–54, New York: Pantheon.

Foucault, M. (2005), *Society Must Be Defended: Lectures at the College De France, 1975–76*, ed. M. Bertani and A. Fontana, trans. D. Macey, London: Penguin.

Frederick, E. L., J. Sanderson and N. Schlereth (2017), 'Kick These Kids Off the Team and Take Away Their Scholarships: Facebook and Perceptions of Athlete Activism at the University of Missouri', *Journal of Issues in Intercollegiate Athletics*, 10: 17–34.

Frost, D. J. (2011), *Seeing Stars: Sports Celebrity, Identity, and Body Culture in Modern Japan*, Cambridge, MA: Harvard University Asia Center.

Gill, E. (2016), '"Hands Up, Don't Shoot" or Shut Up and Play Ball? Fan-Generated Media Views of the Ferguson Five', *Journal of Human Behavior in the Social Environment*, 26 (3–4): 400–12.

Gu, Q. (2014), 'Sina Weibo: A Mutual Communication Apparatus between the Chinese Government and Chinese Citizens', *China Media Research*, 10 (2): 72–85.

Guo, Y. (2004), *Cultural Nationalism in Contemporary China: The Search for National Identity under Reform*, London: Routledge Curzon.

Jackson, S. (2001), 'Gretzky Nation: Canada, Crisis and Americanization', in D. Andrews and S. Jackson (eds) *The Cultural Politics of Sporting Celebrity*, 164–86, London and New York: Routledge.

Jacobs, A. (2009), 'Jackie Chan Strikes a Chinese Nerve', *The New York Times*, 23 April. Available online: http://www.nytimes.com/2009/04/24/world/asia/24jackie.html?_r=0.

Jain, K., I. Sharma and A. Behl (2021), 'Voice of the Stars: Exploring the Outcomes of Online Celebrity Activism', *Journal of Strategic Marketing*, doi: 10.1080/0965254X.2021.2006275.

Jeffreys, E. (2006), 'Debating the Legal Regulation of Sex-related Bribery and Corruption in the People's Republic of China', in E. Jeffreys (ed.), *Sex and Sexuality in China*, 159–78, New York: Routledge.

Jeffreys, E. (2012), 'Modern China's Idols: Heroes, Role Models, Stars and Celebrities', *PORTAL Journal of Multidisciplinary International Studies*, 9 (1): 1–32.

Kaufman, P. (2008), 'Boos, Bans, and Other Backlash: The Consequences of Being an Activist Athlete', *Humanity & Society*, 32 (3): 215–37.

Lee, C. (2003), 'The Global and the National of the Chinese Media: Discourses, Market, Technology, and Ideology', in C. Lee (ed.), *Chinese Media, Global Contexts*, 1–31, London and New York: RoutledgeCurzon.

Li, L. (2001), 'Support for Anti-corruption Campaigns in Rural China', *Journal of Contemporary China*, 10 (29): 573–86.

Meyer, D. (1995), 'The Challenge of Cultural Elites: Celebrities and Social Movements', *Sociological Inquiry*, 65: 181–206.

Sanderson, J., E. Frederick and M. Stocz (2016), 'When Athlete Activism Clashes with Group Values: Social Identity Threat Management via Social Media', *Mass Communication and Society*, 19 (3): 301–22.

Sun, W. (2002), 'Semiotic Over-Determination or "Indoctritainment": Television, Citizenship, and the Olympic Games', in S. Donald, M. Keane and Y. Hong (eds), *Media in China: Consumption, Content and Crisis*, 116–27, London and New York: RoutledgeCurzon.

Thrall, T., J. Lollio-Fakhreddine, J Berent, L. Donnelly, W. Herrin, Z. Paquette, R. Wenglinski and A. Wyatt (2008), 'Star Power: Celebrity Advocacy and the Evolution of the Public Sphere', *Press/Politics*, 13 (4): 362–85.

Vaswati, D. (2012), 'China's Mighty Trip over Mistresses', *Al Jazeera (Qatar)*, posted on 17 June, Available online: https://www.aljazeera.com/features/2012/6/17/chinas-mighty-trip-over-mistresses.

Weiss, A. (2013), '"Mediated Persona" and Hong Kong Stars: Negotiating Mainland Celebrity', *Celebrity Studies*, 4 (2): 219–32.

Wong, C. H. (2020), 'Chinese Sporting Power Couple Issues Rare Rebuke of Ruling Communist Party', *The Wall Street Journal*. Available online: https://www.wsj.com/articles/chinese-sporting-power-couple-issues-rare-rebuke-of-ruling-communist-party-11591797324.

Wu, X. (2007), *Chinese Cyber Nationalism: Evolution, Characteristics, and Implications*, Lanham: Lexington Books.

Wu, Y. (2000), '惩治性贿赂' (Punishing sex-related bribery and corruption), 中国青年报, posted on 13 December.

Xie, D. (2003), '简论性贿赂犯罪立法' (A brief discussion on the criminalization of sex-related bribery and corruption), 安徽律师网, 29 May. Available online: www.ahlawyer.com.cn/kanwu/2003/lx2/more.html.

Yoo, J., H. Lee and Y. Jin (2018), 'Effects of Celebrity Credibility on Country's Reputation: A Comparison of an Olympic Star and a Political Leader', *Corporate Reputation Review*, 21: 127–36.

Chapter 5

Andrews, D. and S. Jackson (2001), 'Introduction: Sport Celebrities, Public Culture, and Private Experience Sport Stars', in D. Andrews and S. Jackson (eds), *The Cultural Politics of Sporting Celebrity*, 1–19, London and New York: Routledge.

Birtles, B. (2021), 'Kris Wu Faces Rape Charges, Triggering Debate on China's #MeToo Movement and Celebrity Culture', *ABC News*, 6 August. Available online: https://www.abc.net.au/news/2021-08-06/china-pop-star-kris-wu-accused-of-rape/100344650.

Chin, B. (2007), 'Beyond Kung-Fu and Violence: Locating East Asian Cinema Fandom', in J. Gray, C. L. Harrington and C. Sandvoss (eds), *Fandom: Identities and Communities in a Mediated World*, 210–19, New York: New York University Press.

'都美竹再爆料吴亦凡信息量大' (2021). Available online: https://finance.sina.cn/2021-07-19/detail-ikqciyzk6219466.d.html.

Dyer, R. (2004), *Heavenly Bodies: Film Stars and Society*, London and New York: Routledge.

Feasey, R. (2008), 'Reading Heat: The Meanings and Pleasures of Star Fashions and Celebrity Gossip', *Continuum: Journal of Media & Cultural Studies*, 22 (5): 687–99.

Gies, L. (2011), 'Stars Behaving Badly', *Feminist Media Studies*, 11 (3): 347–61.

Hunt, P. (2020), 'The Road Home: Rebellion, the Market and Masculinity in the Han Han Phenomenon', *China Perspectives*, (3): 29–37.

Jeffreys, E. (2006), 'Debating the Legal Regulation of Sex-related Bribery and Corruption in the People's Republic of China', in E. Jeffreys (ed.), *Sex and Sexuality in China*, 159–78, New York: Routledge.

Jeffreys, E. and L. Edwards (2010), 'Celebrity/China', in E. Jeffreys and L. Edwards (eds), *Celebrity in China*, 1–20, Hong Kong: Hong Kong University Press.

Johansson, S. (2006), 'Sometimes You Wanna Hate Celebrities: Tabloid Readers and Celebrity Coverage', in S. Holmes and S. Redmond (eds), *Framing Celebrity*, 343–58, London: Routledge.

Lan, L. (2021), 'West's Undisguised Intention of Using MeToo Movement to Create Antagonism in China'. Available online: https://www.globaltimes.cn/page/202109 /1234461.shtml.

'李靓蕾长文原文内容王力宏和李靓蕾离婚原因是什么揭秘' (2021). Available online: http://www.mnw.cn/news/ent/2562531.html.

Marshall, D. (1997), *Celebrity and Power: Fame in Contemporary Culture*, Minneapolis and London: University of Minnesota Press.

Muzi, M. (2004), 遗情书: 我的性爱日记. Available online: http://www.56wen.com/ chapter/20170911/7984.html.

Redmond, S. (2008), 'The Star and Celebrity Confessional', *Social Semiotics*, 18 (2): 109–14.

Redmond, S. (2019), *Celebrity*, London and New York: Routledge.

Ribke, N. (2015), *A Genre Approach to Celebrity Politics: Global Patterns of Passage from Media to Politics*, New York: Palgrave Macmillan.

Savigny, H. and H. Warner (2015), 'Introduction', in H. Savigny and H. Warner (eds), *The Politics of Being a Woman Feminism, Media and 21st Century Popular Culture*, 1–24, London: Palgrave Macmillan.

Turner, G. (2004), *Understanding Celebrity*, London: SAGE.

Weiss, A. (2013), '"Mediated Persona" and Hong Kong Stars: Negotiating Mainland Celebrity', *Celebrity Studies*, 4 (2): 219–32.

Xu, H., J. Zeng, Z. Tai and H. Hao (2022), 'Public Attention and Sentiment toward Intimate Partner Violence Based on Weibo in China: A Text Mining Approach', *Healthcare*, 10: 1–25.

Yang, L. (2009), 'All for Love: The Corn Fandom, Prosumers, and the Chinese Way of Creating a Superstar', *International Journal of Cultural Studies*, 12 (5): 527–43.

'杨丽萍'不生孩子'被群嘲：女性的婚姻与生育都应是自由的' (2020). Available online: https://www.thepaper.cn/newsDetail_forward_7804364.

Yu, S. Q. (2012), 'Vulnerable Chinese Stars: From Xizi to Film Worker', in Y. Zhang (ed.), *A Companion to Chinese Cinema*, 218–38, Malden: Wiley-Blackwell.

Chapter 6

Abidin, C. (2018), *Internet Celebrity: Understanding Fame Online*, Bingley: Emerald Publishing Limited.

'《德國之聲》專訪「李老師不是你老師」：真正偉大的是敢站在街
    上的這些人，我只是被歷史選中的記錄者' (2022). Available online: https://
    www.thenewslens.com/article/177601.
'李佳琦直播被封 促90后找真相 中共陷尷尬' (2022). Available online: https://www
    .epochtimes.com/gb/22/6/6/n13753692.htm.
'李老师不是你老师推特'(2022). Available online：https://twitter.com/
    whyyoutouzhele?ref_src=twsrc%5Egoogle%7Ctwcamp%5Eserp%7Ctwgr
    %5Eauthor.
'李老师不是你老师: 致所有正在找我和准备找我的公职人员' (2022). Available
    online: https://www.aboluowang.com/2022/1129/1835677.html.
'李文亮如果不能写进历史教科书中国还是个尊重历史的国家吗?' (2022).
    Available online: https://www.youtube.com/watch?v=VFQkH1SnG10.
Press-Reynolds, K. (2022), 'China's "Lipstick King" Influencer Li Jiaqi Goes Offline
    after Livestream of a "Tank Cake" Fuels Tiananmen Massacre Talk'. Available
    online: https://news.yahoo.com/chinas-lipstick-king-influencer-li-141535601
    .html.
'勇敢真实的声音非常重要: 陈秋实大年初八中午武汉总结播报' (2020). Available
    online: https://www.youtube.com/watch?v=on8SzRBqZk0&t=806s.
'直击/警人墙镇压! '防疫过当' 新疆大火10死, 上海民众聚乌鲁木齐路高喊习下台
    '两车人被捕" (2022). Available online: https://www.businesstoday.com.tw/article/
    category/183027/post/202211270027/.
'中国活动人士和异见者为何在Twitter上遭压制' (2023). Available online: https://
    cn.nytimes.com/technology/20230216/twitter-china-elon-musk/.

Chapter 7

Meyers, E. (2009), 'Can You Handle My Truth: Authenticity and the Celebrity Star
    Image', *The Journal of Popular Culture*, 42 (5): 890–907.
Nayar, P. K. (2021), *Essays in Celebrity Culture: Stars and Styles*, London: Anthem
    Press.
Redmond, S. (2018), *Celebrity*, London: Taylor & Francis.
'严歌苓：巨大幻灭 十年一觉中国梦 担心自废武功…' (2023). Available online:
    https://www.wenxuecity.com/news/2023/06/28/12390679.html.

Index